Inequality and Flourishing:
A Theology of Education

Inequality and Flourishing

A Theology of Education

Mariama Ifode-Blease

scm press

Published in 2022 by SCM Press
Editorial office
3rd Floor, Invicta House,
108–114 Golden Lane,
London EC1Y 0TG, UK

www.scmpress.co.uk

SCM Press is an imprint of Hymns Ancient & Modern Ltd
(a registered charity)

Hymns Ancient & Modern® is a registered trademark of
Hymns Ancient & Modern Ltd
13A Hellesdon Park Road, Norwich,
Norfolk NR6 5DR, UK

All rights reserved. No part of this publication may be reproduced,
stored in a retrieval system, or transmitted,
in any form or by any means, electronic, mechanical,
photocopying or otherwise, without the prior permission of
the publisher, SCM Press.

The Author has asserted her right under the Copyright, Designs and
Patents Act 1988 to be identified as the Author of this Work

Scripture quotations, unless otherwise indicated, are from
New Revised Standard Version Bible: Anglicized Edition,
copyright © 1989, 1995 National Council of the Churches of
Christ in the United States of America. Used by permission.
All rights reserved worldwide.

British Library Cataloguing in Publication data
A catalogue record for this book is available
from the British Library

978-0-334-06084-0

Typeset by Regent Typesetting

Contents

Preface   ix

Introduction   1
The Empty Tomb Stares Back at Us

Period 1: Assembly   20
The Call to be our Fullest Selves

INTERVIEW WITH MS CAROLINE BRAGGS   34

Period 2: English and Modern Languages   51
Language and Liberation

Period 3: The Arts   76
Living Beyond Words

INTERVIEW WITH REVD CANON DR JOANNA COLLICUTT   93

Period 4: Sports   109
Starting the Race Fairly

Period 5: Science   123
Universal Matter

INTERVIEW WITH PROFESSOR CHRIS JACKSON   138

Period 6: Geography   149
Harvesting Potential

Period 7: Lunch　　　　　　　　　　　　　　165
Eating is a Right not a Privilege

Period 8: History　　　　　　　　　　　　　178
Whose History is it Anyway?

Period 9: Maths　　　　　　　　　　　　　　198
Calculating the Cost

Towards a New Vision for Secondary Education　　218

Names and Subjects Index　　　　　　　　223

For my beloved, Oliver

Preface

This is a book for anyone who is interested in secondary school education in England, not primarily from a policy perspective, but from the viewpoint of how it works for and against children and young people. It is a book written through a Western theological lens, but which seeks to continue a conversation that has been heightened by a global pandemic (Covid-19), which in turn has highlighted the social inequalities and economic and health disparities at local, national and international levels. There is no claim to exclusivity: anyone of any background, belief or creed can subscribe to the desire to see us give the very best in educational terms to our children. This book is not just for those of us with a Christian faith. It couldn't possibly be because of the need to focus not on what separates us, but on the call to improve the lived experience and daily lives of our children, and especially their experience of education. Yet, from my identity as a Black woman of British and Nigerian heritage, an educator, and priest in the Church of England, part of the Anglican Communion, it was important to be authentic to what inspired me to write this book: the belief that we can do better, we can create better, we can imagine better.

The impetus for writing this book is to establish a framework of interrogation for ideas I have had for some time about who and what state education is for, who controls it and what are our expectations of it. Approximately 93 per cent of children across the UK (in 2022) are in state education, so it seemed right and fitting to focus on this part of the sector. In presenting ideas about education, I write as someone deeply interested and invested in the notion of flourishing, particularly for children and young people. As adults, our priority is to ensure that we provide the environments and opportunities for this to occur.

As I write, Covid-19 is still widespread, and its effects continue to be significant in both economically strong and low-medium income nations across the globe. This is not a book necessarily about how secondary education has been defined and brought under scrutiny by the pandemic. Yet, it would be hard to write this book without making mention of how the pandemic upended our lives in 2020, and continues to do so.

The book examines different aspects of secondary school life, exploring in-built inequalities, and questions whether there is room for overturning them for the sake of the future of our children and young people. The framing of the book around the school timetable and day is intentional. It is a structure with which we are all familiar, and which itself needs challenging. Each chapter of this book is framed by a biblical passage, the first starting at the resurrection. The resurrection, much like the pandemic, leaves us with the sensory and cognitive awareness that the impossible has already happened.

Writer Rebecca Solnit, in reflecting on global disasters, states:

> Disasters begin suddenly and never really end. The future will not, in crucial ways, be anything like the past, even the very recent past of a month or two ago. Our economy, our priorities, our perceptions will not be what they were at the outset of this year.[1]

Solnit also speaks of hope. She continues:

> Hope offers us clarity that, amid the uncertainty ahead, there will be conflicts worth joining and the possibility of winning some of them. And one of the things most dangerous to this hope is the lapse into believing that everything was fine before disaster struck, and that all we need to do is return to

PREFACE

things as they were. Ordinary life before the pandemic was already a catastrophe of desperation and exclusion for too many human beings, an environmental and climate catastrophe, an obscenity of inequality. It is too soon to know what will emerge from this emergency, but not too soon to start looking for chances to help decide it. It is, I believe, what many of us are preparing to do.

It is important to remember that things were not fine before the pandemic. And things will not necessarily be fine as we continue to mourn the loss upon loss each one of us has faced, be it loss of a way of life, routine, big and small events, activities and celebrations, employment and loved ones – the greatest loss there is. This book asks whether a new kind of secondary education system can be imagined, one in which the flourishing of the child and young person can be placed at the centre, and in which there are no limits set on what a child can become or achieve. The impossible has already happened and the impossibility of the resurrection is where we begin.

Note

1 Rebecca Solnit, 2020,'"The impossible has already happened": what coronavirus can teach us about hope', *The Guardian*, 7 April.

Introduction

The Empty Tomb Stares Back at Us

Early on the first day of the week, while it was still dark, Mary Magdalene came to the tomb and saw that the stone had been removed from the tomb. So she ran and went to Simon Peter and the other disciple, the one whom Jesus loved, and said to them, 'They have taken the Lord out of the tomb, and we do not know where they have laid him.' Then Peter and the other disciple set out and went towards the tomb. The two were running together, but the other disciple outran Peter and reached the tomb first. He bent down to look in and saw the linen wrappings lying there, but he did not go in. Then Simon Peter came, following him, and went into the tomb. He saw the linen wrappings lying there, and the cloth that had been on Jesus' head, not lying with the linen wrappings but rolled up in a place by itself. Then the other disciple, who reached the tomb first, also went in, and he saw and believed; for as yet they did not understand the scripture, that he must rise from the dead. Then the disciples returned to their homes.
(John 20.1–10)

This book begins at the empty tomb, with the questioning of the status quo and our expectations. Mary Magdalene, Simon Peter and the other disciple did not expect to see an empty tomb. They did not understand this disruption in their logic model, a model which sought to evaluate and measure what had happened over the past seven intense days. Something had happened to the order of things. The tomb that was meant to hold finality reveals something altogether more disturbing. Somehow, and despite the presence of a woman at the tomb, the first to speak to the resurrected Christ, we have created a history and world in which women have been erased and demoted. We have denied and translated the equality presented into a lesser story. Yet, here we are confronted with the reality of the divine encountering human constructions and overcoming them. We are met with the sign and symbol of a new story and a new beginning. We are challenged to review the empirical but to also recognize the mystery. The empty tomb stares at us as a testimony to the liberation of the imagination enabled by the revelation of our identities located in an eternal and cosmic abode.

For me, to write about education, inequality and flourishing is rooted in the mystery of the resurrection of Jesus Christ. Because for such a time as this was Mary Magdalene born. We are not told much of her work and life in the early church, but her presence and purpose here cannot be ignored. Her flourishing is dependent on her fullest self and identity being recognized, affirmed and celebrated. We know that later she will meet the risen Christ and will speak with him. She has learned what it means to be educated, to question and to explore, to learn and to discern, to seek and serve truth and to share the light of love. In being a witness to the resurrection, a new sense of wholeness is revealed. Her identity has been transformed.

The empty tomb speaks of and to the capacity and potential of humans to believe in something greater than ourselves, and to see that there could be something greater *within* ourselves. This is about knowledge resurrected, about the fear of knowing and believing, and the implication of holding on to truth. The other disciple, though he saw the remnants of Jesus' clothing, 'did not go in'. If we believe that Jesus Christ lived, died, was buried and on the third day was raised from the dead, then where is there to hide? We are exposed to an inexplicable reality that holds us accountable to love and restitution and equity and restoration. This reality, of our imagination liberated, of our human experience transformed, of being somehow allowed to stand in the presence of truth and be unafraid, is what makes us whole.

INTRODUCTION

Flourishing

To flourish
(of a person, animal, or other living organism) grow or develop in a healthy or vigorous way, especially as the result of a particularly favourable environment.[1]

When I obtained a place to study for a part-time PhD in the Spanish and Portuguese Department at the University of Cambridge, the departmental secretary wrote to congratulate me. She informed me that I was the first to study part-time in the department and that 'Erasmus would be proud'. Her words have stayed with me, not because I think that Erasmus, linguist and illegitimate son of a priest, would be proud of me, linguist and priest. Rather because the whole thing seems rather implausible. This was not the story I had been told at school when I was expelled at 16 for telling the truth and standing up to a rather annoying and privileged teacher. Somehow the story I was told by some teachers 'that I would never get anywhere in my life' or 'achieve anything with my life' led to post-graduate study at Cambridge and, prior to that, undergraduate study at the University of St Andrews. We are not our beginnings, middles or ends. We are made whole, within a journey that stretches through eternity and has a marked placed here on earth. Somehow the paving stones of a council estate of northwest London where I grew up and those of sixteenth-century Cambridge, where Erasmus lived and taught, became the path under my feet. The narrative of some displeased teachers who were quick to condemn and slow to inspire could not have foreseen this part of the journey ahead.

I write this book because I believe that our children deserve better than what we are currently offering them in terms of secondary education. Our education system needs to recognize that potential is uncapped and limitless in children and young people. Our intellect, imagination and purpose must work together to nurture and enable that potential to grow and reach full flourishing. At an individual level, this requires subscribing to the simple belief that children and young people are important and that, in the journey from childhood through adolescence and to becoming young adults, there should be a recognition of, and investment in, that importance. It is clear that something needs to change because:

> Most of the schools that today's children attend ... were built when prevailing wisdom assumed that children were born to be taught rather than to learn. Which is why, for so many children, the wonder of learning has been replaced by the tedium of trying to remember what they were taught about something which really didn't interest them very much in the first place.[2]

This book is born out of heartache and hope, hope that *we* who are meant to be in charge of all manner of serious institutions, systems and structures can begin to reveal and celebrate the potential of each child and lead them to self-understanding, a recognition of their own capacity to learn and explore, and to develop and mark their own steps towards flourishing. Human flourishing is not an economic imperative but a *soul imperative* that demands our accountability towards, and responsibility for, children to grow and learn, play and live, in safety. The flourishing of children and young people leads to the flourishing of our societies.

The heartache that feeds this book emerges from the realization that we are failing our children and young people. We have been failing them for centuries. We cannot claim that we do not know this, and we cannot deny our role in creating a world in which success and failure are named from a young age in the mind of a child. We blame the child for the inequalities we have engendered in our society. Who they are as children becomes intertwined with whether they can read or write and how fast they can do this and when, and how this foregrounds their future identity. Reading and writing matter as tools to navigate a world constructed by letters and numbers. Yet experiencing nature and the wordless majesty of the world around us are also equally important.

INTRODUCTION

This book seeks to examine how we hold the gift of childhood through secondary education. It is not an academic exposition of the secondary education system in the United Kingdom. Many books have been written on this subject. Rather, it seeks to interrogate our relationship with education, what we see as its purpose, who it serves best and how we can bring it back to the child at the centre. Our understanding of education needs to be decoupled from economic and financial definitions and demands. The need for education, already recognized as a fundamental human right, will need to be realigned with a notion of flourishing that is neither reductive nor competitive. This book presents a new exploration of wholeness and flourishing in the context of education, and with children and young people at the centre. The child's innate curiosity and sense of engagement with the world around them gives us insight into how life can be experienced: with wonder and awe, questioning and delight, and with a deep sense that learning never ends. In this sense, all children are created and born equal, until they meet the inequalities of the world we have created around them.

Inequality

In a talk she gave at Columbia University, Martha Nussbaum set the matter of inequality in larger terms. She remarked that a capability set a standard not just for what human beings can do but also for how society may fail to nourish them. Inequality constricts the capacities of children; they are endowed to relate more fully, to cooperate more deeply than institutions allow.[3]

The secondary education system we currently have is unequal and does not address the needs of all learners. Many would recognize that our current school system at secondary level works for some and not for others. Why is that? Some would say it is as a result of the move from learning more broadly to a narrower concept of education that focuses primarily on testing and exams. Others would cite development and history of secondary education shaped along class boundaries and lines.

Education and class have a long and well-charted history:

> This classed approach to education planning is clearly illustrated through the work and recommendations of the three great school commissions that were set up in the late nineteenth century to examine and make recommendations for the future of educational provision:
> - Newcastle Commission 1861: elementary schools
> - Clarendon Commission 1864: Royal Commission on Public Schools
> - Schools Inquiry Commission 1868 (Taunton Commission): grammar and endowed schools.[4]

We may sometimes take it for granted that the current system is unable to change and that it has always been like that. Yet no human-made system is so set in stone that it cannot be changed at all. If we made it this way, and recognize that it does not work or lend itself to the flourishing of our children and young people, then we can and *should* change it. The 'great school commissions' were a response to the society of the time. There was educational segregation across class lines as reflected in the reports:

> Three separate school systems developed (elementary for the working class, secondary for the middle class and private public schools for the ruling class), and a national system locally controlled and delivered for elementary, then secondary, schools was gradually put in place by a series of Acts in 1870, 1880, 1899 and 1902.[5]

We still live with this legacy today, albeit in a more splintered form. We are not aware of it sometimes and, at other times, we are so aware that what we have created in secondary education overwhelms us and we can see no way forward but to

INTRODUCTION

accept the status quo. The reality is that secondary education was considered a privilege, and only for some. It was never intended for everyone, and it was never meant to be free:

> Compulsion was not introduced for 5- to 10-year-olds until 1881, while provision for 10- to 14- year-olds differed widely around the country. Fees were not abolished until 1891, a move viewed with alarm by many politicians and commentators.[6]

What we have today in terms of free universal secondary education is not the norm in many low-medium countries where fees preclude children and young people from being educated. When a family assesses who should get that education it is often the boy that wins that privilege, with girls not given the opportunity to fulfil their full potential.[7]

The education movement from the late nineteenth to the early twentieth century sought to create a new and more coherent state system that would serve more children, though along class lines. There was a growing sense, too, that education needed to move from being a privilege to becoming a right:

> Nonetheless, the infrastructure of a modern bureaucratic state system of education was gradually established and continued to evolve between 1868 and 1902. Schooling became accepted as a social right, and it was within the field of education that a commitment to universalism first became embedded in state policy.[8]

This movement grew in ambition and purpose, seeking to offer state education for as many children as possible and through a range of options, which wrongly conflated ability with the child's socio-economic environment. The three school commissions of the 1860s still had a clear influence, nonetheless, and this can be seen in one of the most significant pieces of post-second world war legislation:

... While the [1944] Education Act may have established the principle of universal and free secondary education for all, the division into grammar, secondary modern and sometimes technical schools, different types of school for different 'types' of student with different 'types of mind', was clearly again modelled on a class-divided vision of education, albeit a more porous one than previously.[9]

These divisions into different types of schools, known as the 'tripartite system' did not help children, but enabled society to classify and label them. From the 1950s onwards, a hierarchy developed with grammar schools at the top, secondary moderns in the middle and technical schools at the bottom. Yet, 'it soon became clear that the tripartite system largely benefited middle-class children and that selection at 11 was not offering equal opportunities'.[10] The education system as designed was clearly not working. 'Grammar schools became associated with high-status education and secondary moderns as low-status schooling.'[11] 'Rather a means of giving children the appropriate education, the 11-plus came to be a test to be passed or failed – even people today consider themselves failures because they did not pass.'[12] It was easy to see how this had been achieved. The use of the 11-plus only emphasized divisions further as 'children attending secondary modern schools were not given the opportunity to gain qualifications until 1965 when the Certificate of Secondary Education (CSE) was introduced. Selective education reinforced a system and society already fractured by inequalities'.[13] Further, this CSE exam was 'designed for less academically able students who were "not capable" of taking O-levels'.[14] It is clear that there was already a narrative that painted a picture of certain schools being better. What kind of message, therefore, were children and young people receiving in secondary moderns? That they were not good enough to gain qualifications, or certainly not as good or worthy as the children who went to grammar schools. Still, none of this is the child's fault. We continue to

INTRODUCTION

build systems around children that label and limit their potential. And that is on us.

Grammar schools began to be removed in the 1960s to make way for comprehensives, which offered an 'all in one school' for all students. Supporters believed in the idea of 'the "social mix", which looked forward to the amelioration of social class differences through the pupils' experience of "social mixing" in a common secondary school.'[15] The problem, of course, was that some parents did not want this kind of mixing at all and, in fact, preferred the segregation across class lines: 'The removal of grammar schools [in the 1960s] led to an increase in the proportion of the age group attending independent schools and high-achieving pupils being "creamed off" the state sector. This has now stabilised at around 7–8% (Independent Schools Council, 2008).'[16] We now also recognize that the 'system was manipulated by middle-class parents, even to the point of moving house to be within the catchment area of a particular school',[17] which arguably continues to this day.

The reality of this system is that there seemed to be more concern about the type of schools in existence than what was actually being taught in them. The focus on diversifying school provision, which sought to bring children and young people together from across society meant that less attention was paid to learning:

> The reports which followed the growth of comprehensives in the 1950s, 1960s and 1970s did not examine issues of pedagogy, selection and assessment, which meant that the majority of comprehensives 'simply attempted to assimilate the two existing curriculum traditions handed down from the grammar and secondary modern schools'.[18]

This quest for plurality in provision has continued through to the beginnings of the twenty-first century. Since the 1960s, successive governments have moved power away from local authorities who used to manage schools, to schools themselves, to philanthropists, trusts, religious and other organizations who manage secondary schools across England. It is a confusing and somewhat complicated picture:

> Tomlinson[19] comments that by January 2000 the drive towards a diverse educational system had led to 13 kinds of schooling: independent schools, grammar schools, church and faith schools, specialist schools, advanced specialist schools, city academies, city technology colleges, 'fresh start' schools, 'contract' schools, trust schools and some comprehensives and secondary moderns.[20]

We can now add free schools, city technology colleges and state boarding schools to the list.[21] Most parents and carers, regardless of the school chosen for their child, want their child to be safe, happy and to enjoy their school years. Of course, parents and carers will also want their children to learn things and develop their minds. The state education system we now have, it could be argued, is more focused on testing than learning and it is to this idea that we now turn.

Testing and examinations

I hated exams and testing at school, and at university. I remember not sleeping very well before my GCSE exams and not feeling as if I would do well. I was able to overcome the combination of anxiety, fear and nerves to do well in them, and did the same again at A level. At university, I was able to manage to perform on the day, despite the internal mental challenges. Exams and testing take an emotional and psychological toll on our children and young people, and we have to continue to interrogate who exactly it serves to tell children and young people, whether knowingly or unknowingly, that their worth and intellectual and potential capacity are based on tests and exams.

INTRODUCTION

As a result of the pandemic, 2021 was the second year in which national General Certificate of Secondary Education (GSCE) exams, taken at aged 16, and Advance Level (A level), taken at aged 18, did not happen. In June 2020:

> A campaign between state and private schools plans to launch a manifesto to end GCSE exams, branded by Lord Kenneth Baker as based on an 'Edwardian' curriculum. In a meeting of the group last week, Lord Baker, the former education secretary who helped introduce GCSEs, said he thought the exams had 'run their course.'[22]

The unification of both state and private sectors over the scrapping of GCSEs speaks volumes for the growing sense of displeasure at the testing and exams regime our children are subjected to at 16 and 18 years of age. These forms of assessment do not work for all children with their focus on recalling specific information, even more specific exam technique and working under intense pressure. The exams, while they may offer some insights into future academic potential, in no way account for the full potential of any child and can in no way predict future success or happiness.

This testing regime is of course linked to the National Curriculum (NC), introduced in the 1988 Education Reform Act:

> 1988 was a milestone date, with the passing of the education Reform Act, which from 1989 introduced a National Curriculum (NC) for the first time. This NC was conventionally structured with three core subjects (mathematics, English and science) and seven foundation subjects.[23]

While the National Curriculum enabled a standardized offering to subject content and knowledge, it invariably meant that teachers and learners were locked into its prescriptive, hierarchical presentation of which subjects matter and which do not. Academies and free schools are not obliged to follow the NC, but this is a false sense of freedom as they in effect have to follow the NC in order for their students to be able to meet the demands of testing and exams that are still based on that curriculum. The fact is, an imposed curriculum enables measuring and comparison, and emphasizes testing and examinations over a more expansive love of learning as well as intellectual and creative curiosity:

> In summary, there is a subject focused NC with high stakes accountability, driven by national testing and school inspections which have focused overwhelmingly on test results, inspired by neoliberal market ideology which identifies competition between schools as the key process to improve education.[24]

So, we can see that there is a great challenge before us. It encompasses unlocking the potential of educators to be allowed to teach with real passion and a love for their subjects, creating engaging and contextually relevant curriculum, and for students to be enabled to build a sustained and positive relationship with learning that affirms their potential.

We have created a system that perpetuates itself. Testing and exams have come to define what success means and looks like for schools and generations of students, and to move away from them would leave students feeling misled at best and set up to fail, at worst:

> With a dominant discourse in England which promotes a view of a successful education as passing exams, getting good grades and then going to university, it is understandable that students in this climate feel under intense pressure to demonstrate 'success' in this way. For the students to accept that they are capable of learning enough to pass an exam through their own efforts would require a shift in their 'epistemological perspective' away from the teacher as the font of all knowledge.[25]

INTRODUCTION

Furthermore, children grow up to expect testing and exams, to focus and prepare for them at the cost of exploring other interests and passions, and to anchor their measurement of success to the results that they receive. Our education system creates a dependency on learning to pass a test or exam and is almost designed to be fearful of the thinking child and young person:

> So what happens to that wanting-to-know instinct? Do schools create an environment that encourages profound questions and independent thinking as children seek to sort out what is for them merely a routine or a distraction? If humans are, by nature, a learning species, do schools build on that potential and work with the grain of the brain, or do they so work against it that they roughen up the surface and cause deep internal haemorrhaging?[26]

It is important to stress, once more, that none of this is of the child's making, or the teachers', for that matter. A good teacher will be wholeheartedly committed to the flourishing of children and young people. It is also fair to say that a good teacher may not be allowed to fully engage with their own commitment to learning and to their students' because the system does not allow them to be. Simply put, the current education system suffocates teachers.

So, we have a secondary education system that locks children and young people in an unnecessary and harmful cycle of testing and exams, that also locks teachers into a prescriptive pedagogy and curriculum and schools that are locked into an inspection regime that gives little room to reprioritize and refocus on a child-centred, whole-person philosophy of education:

> In the new inspection regime (Ofsted 2019), three terms hold most attention: intent, implementation and impact. Intent requires schools to offer a rich and varied curriculum, going beyond test requirements, implementation requires a strong focus on subjects and subject knowledge but with

strong elements of discussion and engagement, while impact requires that knowledge is retained in long term memory with an effect too on behaviour and attitudes. There is also some renewed emphasis on the whole person in a new section in the framework on 'Personal Development'. This section diversifies the curriculum taking in the need to discover talents and interests, develop resilience and character, be responsible citizens and maintain physical and mental health. So, while this section reflects liberal concerns about the whole person, crucially the inspectors only comment on provision and not impact and therefore this section has less leverage than subject knowledge and its retention in memory, which is explicitly referred to as cultural capital.[27]

What we see, therefore, is a system that traps children and young people, teachers and schools. The inspection regime only serves to pay lip-service to a broader concept of education while its focus remains on subject knowledge and the ability to recall and regurgitate information. This is the impact of education that is examined and inspected. Schools cannot, therefore, be asked to 'go beyond test requirements' and focus on 'Personal Development' if those tests and exams are the basis on which they are truly judged.

It is difficult not to see all of this 'as part of a neoliberal process of change, schools are being encouraged and required to become more like and to act more like business'.[28] The concept of subject knowledge and a focus on knowledge acquisition link education to the financial system in which we operate and to the idea of a knowledge economy, which 'derives from the idea that knowledge and education can be treated as a business product, and that educational and innovative intellectual products and services, as productive assets, can be exported for a high-value return'.[29] We need to decouple education from market and financial imperatives and return to the prioritization of the flourishing of children and young people. We need to re-evaluate how we measure success not only in education, but also in our wider society.

INTRODUCTION

Our education system, it must be said, does not exist in a vacuum. Inasmuch as it has been the product of social inequalities across the past two centuries, in its current form, it also reflects the impact of globalization on the sector. We see this in the plurality of provision for example, in who leads, funds and runs our schools:

> In England philanthropic foundations are now active across a range of new education policy initiatives such as academy and free schools sponsorships and Teach First.[30] Some of these national actors are also exporting their policy ideas to other countries (like ARK to India and parts of Africa). Teach for All, which began in the US as Teach for America, now operates in 40 countries around the world and is primarily funded by business foundations.[31]

It is important to recognize the impact of the world beyond our shores on our education system to better understand how it lives, moves and has its being. Successive governments have sought to compare and contrast the secondary education system with others across the world, seeking to adopt best practice or replicate pedagogic models. The principal source for this competitive and often nationalistic assessment of education is the Organisation for Economic Co-operation and Development (OECD), which 'operates through a form of rational peer pressure to disseminate "what works" in policy terms, in particular, policies that have proved to be "successful" responses to international competition – again, the primacy of the economic imperative'.[32] This again emphasizes how the notion of education has become so intertwined with the economy. There is a greater challenge, too, because the comparison with nation states is a regular feature of and reason for government interference in the education systems:

> Perhaps the most powerful of the OECD's policy instruments has been the three-yearly Programme for International Student Assessment (PISA) study results (first published in

2003) in which over 80 countries have now participated (www.pisa.oed.org/). PISA testing is a major income stream for the OECD and a considerable cost to participating nations ... UK education ministers frequently refer to PISA scores and comparisons with other countries in their speeches, and also repeatedly use OECD reports and studies as points of reference and forms of legitimation for their policies, when these suit their purposes.[33]

The idea that education can be more than the production of an individual to fit into an economic structure is lost in the system we have created. What seems to matter most is not the flourishing of a child or young person but the creation of 'education policies [that] are formed and developed in relation to the supposed pressures of international economic competition; other purposes or outcomes from education are threatened with subordination to economic "necessities"'.[34] What it means to be educated, therefore, is reduced to what can be measured within this model of economic competition and these economic imperatives. Rather 'the meaning of education and what it means "to be educated" are changed and a new kind of flexible, lifelong learner is articulated by policy as human capital in relation to the knowledge economy'.[35] There is no sense here that what it means to be educated relates to the liberation of the mind and person, to enable a person to fulfil their full potential, to teaching and learning underpinned by a moral compass that speaks to and promotes the common good. As the letter below reminds us, education cannot and must never simply be seen in reductive and narrow terms. The letter was 'sent by an American high school principal to all his newly appointed teachers on the first day of each new academic year':

Dear Teacher,
I am a survivor of a concentration camp. My eyes saw what no man should witness. Gas chambers built by learned engineers. Children poisoned by educated physicians. Infants

killed by trained nurses. Women and babies shot and burned by high school and college graduates. So, I am suspicious of education.

My request is: help your students to become human. Your efforts must never produce learned monsters, skilled psychopaths, educated Eichmanns. Reading, writing, arithmetic are all important; but only if they serve to make our children more human.[36]

Reimagining the education system

It is time to reimagine the education system, given that we are now almost a quarter of the way through the twenty-first century. The reality is that, 'in some ways, we end [this chapter] where we began, with a disarticulated education system made up of many routes and diverse providers'.[37] The multiple emphases on the providers, on who owns the school, who controls the school, who funds the school and what should be taught in it have all bypassed the fundamental and central focus on the child and young person, and on their flourishing.

In order to bring the secondary education system to where it needs to be, it should be better funded and resourced for child-centred and whole person education. The culture of testing and exams needs to be interrogated, with the scrapping of national exams and testing throughout, and the exploration of new ways of assessing learning and understanding that affirm the child's potential. There needs to be a review of the National Curriculum, its contents and purpose and new measurements of success introduced into our education system. The National Curriculum needs to tell the multiple stories of our island and be truthful in its representation of its past and present. A more localized form of curriculum that promotes core themes could be explored, that locates the child in their community but also expands their mind to other communities and ways of life. Teachers should be enabled to bring their creativity and love of their subjects back into the classrooms, to have the space to have fun and play with learning, without the fear of being judged against the metrics of test and exam results.

The notion of learning, and the enjoyment of learning, has to be re-emphasized and brought back to the core of our education system. Learning that puts the child's and young person's imagination, creativity and curiosity at the centre of the process, and seeks to nurture and nourish these. We need an education system that cares about our children and young people, that provides varied pathways of engagement and learning, that blends the practical and theoretical, and that points to the possibilities of how they can inhabit their place in the world.

Notes

1 Lexico, 'Flourish', *Lexico*, www.lexico.com/en/definition/flourish, accessed 29.04.2021.

2 John Abbott with Heather MacTaggart, 2010, *Over schooled but Undereducated: How the Crisis in Education is Jeopardizing our Adolescents*, London and New York: Continuum, p. 9.

3 Richard Sennett, 2013, *Together*, London: Penguin, p. 146.

4 Stephen J. Ball, 2017, *The Education Debate*, Bristol: Policy Press, p. 68.

5 Ball, *The Education Debate*, p. 69.

6 Ball, *The Education Debate*, p. 70.

7 Girlup, https://girlup.org/issues/education, accessed 01.05.2021.

8 Ball, *The Education Debate*, p. 71.

9 Ball, *The Education Debate*, p. 75.

10 Stephen Ward and Christine Eden, 2009, *Key Issues in Education Policy*, London: Sage Publications, p. 35.

11 The Newsom Report, 1963, available from www.educationengland.org.uk/documents/newsom/newsom1963.html, accessed 01.05.2021.

12 Ward and Eden, *Key Issues in Education Policy*, p. 35.

13 Ward and Eden, *Key Issues in Education Policy*, p. 35.

14 Ball, *The Education Debate*, p. 78.

15 Clyde Chitty, 2014 (3rd edn), *Education Policy in Britain*, London: Red Globe Press, p. 13.

16 Ward and Eden, *Key Issues in Education Policy*, pp. 36–7.

17 Ward and Eden, *Key Issues in Education Policy*, pp. 37.

INTRODUCTION

18 Chitty, *Education Policy in Britain*, p. 14, also quoted in Ward and Eden, *Key Issues in Education Policy*, p. 44.
19 Sally Tomlinson, 2015 (2nd edn), *Education in a Post-Welfare Society*, Buckingham: Open University, p. 103.
20 Ward and Eden, *Key Issues in Education Policy*, p. 39.
21 UK Government, 'Types of school', *Gov.uk*, www.gov.uk/types-of-school, accessed 01.05.2021.
22 TES Magazine, 'State and private schools in "movement" to scrap GCSEs', *TES Magazine*, www.tes.com/news/state-and-private-schools-movement-scrap-gcses, accessed 01.05.2021.
23 Gemma Parker and David Leat, 2021, 'The Case of Curriculum Development in England: Oases in a Curriculum Desert' in Mark Priestley, Daniel Alvunger, Stavroula Philippou and Tiina Soini (eds), *Curriculum Making in Europe: Policy and Practice Within and Across Diverse Contexts*, Bingley: Emerald Publishing, pp. 151–74, p. 152.
24 Parker and Leat, 'The Case of Curriculum Development in England: Oases in a Curriculum Desert', p. 153. See also Carl Bagley, 2006, 'School Choice and Competition: A Public-Market in Education Revisited', *Oxford Review of Education*, 32(3), pp. 347–62.
25 Parker and Leat, 'The Case of Curriculum Development in England: Oases in a Curriculum Desert', p. 165.
26 Abbott and MacTaggart, *Over schooled but Undereducated*, pp. 21–2.
27 Parker and Leat, 'The Case of Curriculum Development in England: Oases in a Curriculum Desert', p. 154.
28 Ball, *The Education Debate*, p. 18.
29 Ball, *The Education Debate*, p. 25.
30 See also: Patrick Bailey, 2015, 'Consultants of conduct: new actors, new knowledges and new "resilient" subjectivities in the governing of the teacher', *Journal of Educational Administration and History*, 47(3), pp. 232–50.
31 Ball, *The Education Debate*, p. 33.
32 Ball, *The Education Debate*, p. 40.
33 Ball, *The Education Debate*, p. 41.
34 Ball, *The Education Debate*, p. 46.
35 Ball, *The Education Debate*, p. 46.
36 Cited in Richard Prin, 1984, *Personal and Social Education in the Curriculum*, Sevenoaks: Hodder and Stoughton, p. viii and again in Clyde Chitty, *Education Policy in Britain*, p. 238.
37 Ball, *The Education Debate*, p. 116.

Period 1: Assembly

The Call to be our Fullest Selves

As Jesus passed along the Sea of Galilee, he saw Simon and his brother Andrew casting a net into the sea – for they were fishermen. And Jesus said to them, 'Follow me and I will make you fish for people.' And immediately they left their nets and followed him. As he went a little farther, he saw James son of Zebedee and his brother John, who were in their boat mending the nets. Immediately he called them; and they left their father Zebedee in the boat with the hired men, and followed him.
(Mark 1. 16–20)

It is an extraordinary thing to be seen and recognized in the routine of daily life, to be brought forward from regular and familiar tasks and be asked to look beyond them to a greater purpose within and beyond yourself. There is something of these leaps in vision and of the imagination in this story. Jesus could see and recognize potential not marked against a rigidity of a formulaic assessment but emerging from the work that was already being done and the lives already being lived.

What was it about the fishermen that made Jesus pause? Was it the way in which they worked collaboratively, their concentration or level of commitment? Was it their talking and laughter and insider jokes? Whatever he saw, he made his case in a few words and the fishermen were enthralled.

When Jesus calls Simon and Andrew, he interrupts their daily lives, their work, and dedication to family and community. This is not a clear and necessarily joyful call into an adventure, but rather a troubling and arresting invitation. The brothers may have known of Jesus or his father's workshop,

PERIOD I: ASSEMBLY

or his family connections, but was that really enough to jeopardize their livelihood upon which many surely depended? I imagine the emotions they were feeling: some frustration at being interrupted, curiosity and confusion at his words, a tinge of excitement about what would happen next, fear at leaving their work behind, about who would continue it, and the cost implications of their impulsive act.

As hard as I try, I find it difficult to imagine that Simon and Andrew walked behind Jesus in reverential silence. Could a mix of incredulous chortles and daringly pointed questions have danced in the air around them? By the time Jesus reached the sons of Zebedee, there was enough energy (and possibly noise and excitement?) around the group to inspire James and John to leave their father and the hired staff to follow Jesus. I imagine their parents were not impressed at this shirking of familial responsibility.

Jesus called the first two fishermen while they were 'casting a net into the sea' and the brothers while they were 'mending the nets'. The first pair of disciples already had a course of action when they were called. Jesus meets them right in the middle of things, and he calls them to turn away from what they were doing and to turn towards him. According to Mark's account, James and John had not even started, when Jesus interrupts their day. Here he pre-empts a course of action; Jesus calls them to re-evaluate what they are currently doing and to walk with him instead. It was the right voice, at the right time. In both cases, too, we see that Jesus waits; he waits for the men to come to shore from their boats, to disentangle themselves from their nets and work, to move into a space of being and a new way of living.

The sense of adventure as both the group of disciples and Jesus' reputation grew must have been palpable. There is much evidence in all the gospels to show the disciples lack of understanding about what this new journey with this man called Jesus would mean; the challenges it would bring, and the cost of responding to his voice on that pivotal day by the Sea of Galilee. We, too, cannot see the vicissitudes of our walk, in faith. We cannot see our own potential. What the call of the first disciples offers us is the clear image of a God who sees us fully, who interrupts but does not impose, waits but does not admonish, calls, but does not abandon.¹

The role and purpose of education

Education should seek to work towards the child and young person's fullest self. While secondary education does not last for more than five years (or seven if you count the ages 16–18), it intersects with years of monumental importance in terms of adolescent growth and development:

> Young people, especially adolescents, are caught up in the vortex of this whirling mass of conflicting expectations and aspiration. The most stunning change for adolescents today is actually their aloneness – it may not seem like that when you listen to their excited chattering, but beyond their own peer group there is less intergenerational connection now than there has ever been. They talk endlessly to one another, but to the rest of society they remain that tribe apart. This is not because they necessarily come from parents who don't care, or from schools that don't care, or from communities that don't want to value them, but rather because there hasn't been time for adults to lead them through the process of growing up. Youngsters of today are growing up in a world in which the values of mutuality and reciprocity that were once an integral part of British life have been overwhelmed by a shoulder-shrugging individualism that excuses most adults, and society as a whole, from what we used to think of as the responsibility to respect, nurture and support youngsters as they gradually edge into adulthood.²

Anyone who has worked with secondary students understands these words. For all their *joie de vivre* they are still fragile and remain incredibly precious as individuals and as a group. Every generation seems to ask: what is the purpose of education? What is clear is that we currently live with a stagnant and reductive view of education that prioritizes tests and exams over learner-led enquiry and contextual and experiential learning. Children and young people are locked into limited definitions of success that become intertwined with their own definitions of self and self-worth. Much like Abbott and MacTaggart, Martin Luther King Jr, in one of his undergraduate essays, points to the purpose of education being about more than utilitarian. Education, he writes:

> ... must also train one for quick, resolute and effective thinking. To think incisively and to think for one's self is very difficult. We are prone to let our mental life become invaded by legions of half-truths, prejudices, and propaganda ... To save man from the morass of propaganda, in my opinion, is one of the chief aims of education. Education must enable one to sift and weigh evidence, to discern the true from the false, the real from the unreal, and the facts from the fiction.
>
> The function of education, therefore, is to teach one to think intensively and to think critically. But education which stops with efficiency may prove the greatest menace to society. The most dangerous criminal may be the man gifted with reason, but with no morals.[3]

There is something about education, therefore, that should aim for higher ideals and transformative change in the mind. Education should also seek to look beyond the individual for contribution to the common good. We find ourselves in a position where education means very little if it is only focused on recalling information over and over and under pressures in tests and exams. How will that help us confront the global challenges we currently face?

The assembly, character education and British values

I have few memories of exciting or inspiring assemblies from secondary school. They played a part in celebrating achievement: the giving of certificates, the awarding of pins and badges. They also allowed teachers to promote the mission and ethos of the school, which often centred around us being 'good, hard-working girls'. The place of school assemblies is recognized nationally and internationally. UNICEF, for example, has produced a guide for leading and delivering primary school assemblies.[4] There are countless resources available online and in print to help teachers structure their assemblies and get the most out of them. Assemblies offer an open stage upon which schools can place an 'act of worship', a talk, notices, tellings-off, careers education (often at a superficial and performative level), fire drills and emergency evacuations and whatever else the senior leadership team foist on that early morning 10–20-minute slot. Perhaps this is why assemblies have become a natural home for promoting 'British values' and 'character education', whereby speakers offer stories of overcoming obstacles and challenging preconceptions to inspire the students who feel that they probably have better things to do.

In 2018, Rabbi Jonathan Sacks presented a series entitled 'Morality in the 21st Century' on BBC Radio 4, comprising six episodes. In the sixth and final episode, following the pattern of all previous episodes, Rabbi Sacks interviewed a range of thinkers and a group of sixth form students. In it, he explored the idea of 'Moral Heroes': who are they, how are they formed and what impact they have on our lives. Rabbi Sacks argued that as a society 'we have outsourced morality to the market and the state; the state gives us choices and the state deals with the consequences of those choices'. There appears, however, to be a vacuum in judgement, given society's 'increased secularity'. The question of who or what guides our decision-making gave the episode its focus and title ('Moral Heroes').

The Times Education Supplement (18 September 2016) published an article titled, 'The problem with character education'.

In it, the writer argued that, while character education had been wholeheartedly adopted by the Department for Education, few had asked 'whether we really know what character education is – and if "character" is even something that can be taught'. This was despite the research report published in 2015 by the University of Birmingham's Jubilee Centre for Character and Virtues.[5] This report presented character education as a response to societal fragmentation and unravelling. It read 'there is a growing consensus in Britain that virtues such as honesty, self-control, fairness, gratitude and respect, which contribute to good moral character, are part of the solution to many of the challenges facing society today'.[6] The research involved 10,207 students and 255 teachers across the UK, and its aim was to explore 'the nature, impact and current understandings of education for character in British schools, and how such education can be improved'.[7] Kim Allen and Anna Bull have, however, analysed the policy drivers behind the development of character education in the UK highlighting how 'existing critiques of character education describe how it serves a broadly conservative neoliberal political agenda, obscuring structural conditions through a focus on individual behaviour as a solution to education and social problems'.[8] It is important to underline a simple truth: the stark inequalities and the increasing gap between rich and poor is not, nor has it ever been, the fault of the individual.

This emphasis on character, as is often presented in school assemblies, shifts the sense of responsibility from the collective to the individual. It speaks to Rabbi Sacks' suggestion that morality has been 'outsourced' and attempts to address this through a focus on individual self-amelioration through structured interventions within the frameworks of formal learning, as represented by educational institutions. We have to recognize some of the political impetus behind the discourses around 'character'. Some would cite the creation of a 'character education network map' which reveals that:

Much of the evidence in support of character education in the UK comes from university research centres that have received significant funding from the US-based Christian neoconservative John Templeton Foundation ... The JTF's funding for research has played a significant role in the legitimation and development of character education policy within the UK.[9]

The Jubilee Centre for Character and Virtues at the University of Birmingham 'as of June 2017 ... received in excess of £16 million of JTF funding, comprising over 98% of its grant income'.[10] This is important to note because, and I write this as a Christian, the formation of character or the composition of character education is not exclusive to Christianity. Nor should Western theology in its arrogance claim to be the home of character education, however it is defined.

The report 'Character Education in UK Schools' (2015) found that a whole-school approach that incorporated character education, was key. This is probably why and how this character education became such a part of the school day and week. It also highlighted the fact that 'only 33% of teachers stated that they had specific or additional training in moral or character education, yet 60% stated that they had to teach a subject relating explicitly to the development of the whole child (i.e., citizenship)'.[11] This implies that the content of character education is also diffused across different subjects (for example, citizenship, theology or religious studies), though educators may not feel equipped to deliver teaching on character.

History of character education in the UK

Some cite the Scottish Enlightenment of the eighteenth and nineteenth centuries as a useful historical marker because of its focus on 'the study of character in human beings'.[12] That study of character clearly had limited, if any, impact on Scottish businessmen who benefited hugely from the transatlantic

PERIOD 1: ASSEMBLY

slave trade and who bought, sold and owned human beings across North America and the Caribbean. In the Victorian period, character education was developed further. As one scholar writes:

> The Victorian period was certainly a high point in character education, or perhaps more accurately the use of the language of character. The Victorians meant many things by the use of 'character' and many of these meanings did not apply to schooling ... The theory of character formation they operated led to much ambiguity and contradiction in behaviour.[13]

The movement from the idea that character could be formed not only by laws, institutions and social expectations but by schools developed in this period. The English private school, and their headmasters, began to promote the 'educational ideal of "noble character"'.[14] One could argue that it has been hard to identify this idea of noble character in the ruling class and the leaders of successive governments. What is clear is that character education policy is not new, emerging from the 1949 Ministry of Education publication entitled *Citizens Growing Up: At Home, At School and After*[15] and continuing in various iterations until its re-emergence in the 2000s.

The development of character education has been underpinned by virtue ethics and Christian virtue ethics, with virtue being defined as:

> A trait of character or intellect that is in some way praiseworthy, admirable or desirable ... Probably every society has identified certain human characteristics as being especially praiseworthy and worth cultivating, while also identifying others as vices which are morally corrupt, contemptible or otherwise undesirable.[16]

Yet virtue ethics 'treats ethics as concerned with one's whole life – and not just those occasions when something with a distinctly "moral" quality is at stake'.[17] Arguably, this problematizes the notion of character education in schools as its teaching may be reductive. The indirect suggestion is that character is a subject that can be taught and learned, and knowledge of it can be reproduced in summative assessment, in the same way as other curriculum subjects, as opposed to a process of lifelong learning and engagement with 'eudaimonism' and the question 'what is the best way to live?'[18]

Crucially, we live in a world:

> in which our values appear to be constantly changing, and in which children are presented with all kinds of models and exposed to all kinds of opinions about right and wrong. For some, this appears to necessitate a content-based moral education curriculum that many others have rejected as too problematic.[19]

David Brooks in his book *The Road to Character* challenges the imperatives of curricula that focus on the production of outputs, which are both measurable and tangible. He presents two key concepts:

> Résumé virtues and eulogy virtues. The résumé virtues are the ones you list on your résumé, the skills that you bring to the job market and that contribute to external success. The eulogy virtues are deeper. They're the virtues that get talked about at your funeral, the ones that exist at the core of your being – whether you are kind, brave, honest or faithful; what kind of relationships you formed.[20]

His book, in essence, presents historical role models that display through their lives, decisions and actions, eulogy virtues. In the radio broadcast with Rabbi Sacks, Brooks suggests that 'public conversation is over-politicized and under-moralized'. By this he means that public discourse often focuses on political messaging and point-scoring without exploring the moral implications of discussions. If, as Brooks implies, the education system focuses on résumé virtues, it is easy to see why character education has been seen as a useful antidote for broadening and deepening discussion around an ethical praxis for young people.

Brooks, argues, nevertheless, that 'we are more moved by the narrative of a person that we can copy than we are by anything else ... by arguments'. Rabbi Sacks, too, explores the idea of role models with the sixth form students with whom he is in conversation. He argues that, because many young people find religion 'out of step with where people are today', role models represent an opportunity to become educators, stepping into the breech, to address and respond to the ethical questioning by young people who look up to them. For me, the breadth of role models chosen by students (Marie Colvin, Kae Tempest, Emma Watson, Margaret Thatcher, Barack Obama, Madonna, a student's grandmother, another student's single mother, the Emergency Services) indicates the important role prominent figures in different sectors of society play in shaping the conceptualization of 'eulogy virtues'. Teaching and learning around ethics are constantly occurring in public, deregulated, de-institutionalized spaces. The impact of this may be a more individualized ethical praxis for young people. Yet, based on the limited evidence of the role models the students chose, there is a clear indication that the students' understanding of their place in society involves a connection with, and serving within, a community. Their ethical praxis is being shaped by the lives of the role models they are choosing.

Finally, if we contend that role models play an influential part in the ethical praxis of young people what can the scriptures offer in this regard? We know that the 'Hebrew Scriptures do present distinctive ideals of character, especially in the wisdom literature',[21] while the writings of Paul in the New Testament focus on 'character traits'. The person of Jesus Christ has also served as a role model for later Christian thinkers who 'have drawn on New Testament images of Jesus and of the early church to identify other distinctively Christian virtues (e.g., humility)'.[22] We return, however, to the issue highlighted by Rabbi Sacks at the beginning of his programme: secularization of society has led to new 'moral heroes' as the choices of the students on the programme attest.

In examining character education in the secondary school system, and analysing some of the policy drivers and political agenda behind its development, it is clear that it emphasizes the individual and shifts the debate away from wider, collective societal responses to ethical concerns. The history of character education in the UK reveals that this is nothing new. Likewise, there seems to be a tension between a longer engagement with the idea of a 'eudaimonism' and more task- or exercise-focused learning about ethics within a classroom setting. So, character education is squeezed into assembly time and other lessons across the curriculum. Like many other subjects, children and young people are offered a de-contextualized experience, and a codified, curriculum-based character education. The argument Brooks presents is that we are more influenced by people whose lives we admire than by arguments (in a classroom). The influence and impact of character education on the ethical praxis of secondary students, in England at least, is limited given (arguably) the possible wider impact of role models that the students may choose themselves, and from whom they will develop their moral questioning and responses. It is also important to recognize that, even with character education, there seems to be a link to productivity and economic demands:

> The recent revival of interest in character education has generated a plethora of approaches and resources, ranging from materials embedded in the neo-Aristotelian virtue ethics developed by the Jubilee Centre for Character and Virtues, to techniques for the regulation of negative emotions offered by Positive Psychology. Seligman's[23] Positive Psychology and Goleman's[24] Emotional Intelligence models focus on 'positive' character traits aimed at increasing motivation and productivity. The Jubilee Centre embraces a broader approach, by promoting moral, civic, intellectual and performance virtues (Arthur et al., 2015). Policymakers' interest in character education has led to the development of a very

specific formula for 'producing' the desirable character by inculcating, in the English context, the new 'three Rs' of education: resilience, respect and responsibility. This narrowing down of 'character' from the more broadly conceived virtues that, in line with neo-Aristotelian thinking, enable full human flourishing, to the purely instrumentalist goal of improved performance, is indicative of the priority of performativity in English education policy. The introduction of the 'fundamental British values' of democracy, the rule of law, individual liberty and mutual respect and tolerance of those with different faiths and beliefs can be seen as an attempt to regain social cohesion, lost as a result of an increasing individualisation of social relations and other problems characteristic of 'new capitalism'.[25]

Reimagining the school assembly

How could the assembly speak to and give a platform for children and young people in the school? What if school assemblies looked outward instead of offering internal recognition, celebrating some students and ignoring others? What if we took half of the assemblies in a week to dedicate to a social action and social justice programme, where children and young people identified the issues in their local community that affected them and had a negative impact on their lives? What if the mornings in school taught young people how to take responsibility for and participate in the democracy in which they live? The assembly slot could be used for creating youth citizen's assemblies in which every learner would be called upon to contribute and share their opinions, ideas and solutions. There would be support and oversight from a member of the senior leadership team who could act as the liaison between the school and external partners within and beyond the community, to enable the children and young people to form a coalition for change. Schools could collaborate if students felt that their issues warranted a greater level of support within the community. This reimagining of school assemblies would enable experiential and contextual learning roots in their local surroundings in which the children and young people are active agents for change. The school assembly could have at its core the development of an understanding of what it means to be more human, within an interdependent and connected world.

Notes

1 Adapted from the Bible study written for *Magnet* No. 113, summer 2017.

2 John Abbott with Heather MacTaggart, 2010, *Over schooled but Undereducated: How the Crisis in Education is Jeopardizing our Adolescents*, London and New York: Continuum, p. 183. Abbott and MacTaggart, p. 289, point to Elliott Currie, 2004, *The Road to Whatever: Middle-class Culture and the Crisis of Adolescence*, New York: Metropolitan Books, p. 13, and especially chapters 3 and 6 and pp. 262 and 272.

3 Martin Luther King Jr, 1947, 'The Purpose of Education', available from https://kinginstitute.stanford.edu/king-papers/documents/purpose-education, accessed 28.02.2022.

4 UNICEF UK, 'Primary School Assemblies', Unicef, www.unicef.org.uk/rights-respecting-schools/wp-content/uploads/sites/4/2019/06/Primary-School-Assemblies-200619.pdf, accessed 30.04.2021.

5 James Arthur, Kristján Kristjánsson, et al., 2015, *Character Education in UK Schools: Research Report*, Birmingham: University of Birmingham's Jubilee Centre for Character and Virtues.

6 Arthur and Kristjánsson, et al., *Character Education in UK Schools: Research Report*, p. 5

7 Arthur and Kristjánsson, et al., *Character Education in UK Schools: Research Report*, p. 7

8 Kim Allen and Anna Bull, 2018, 'Following Policy: A Network Ethnography of the UK Character Education Policy Community', *Sociological Research Online*, 23(2), pp. 438–58, p. 439.

9 Allen and Bull, 'Following Policy: A Network Ethnography of the UK Character Education Policy Community', p. 442.

10 Allen and Bull, 'Following Policy: A Network Ethnography of the UK Character Education Policy Community', p. 443.

11 Arthur and Kristjánsson, et al., *Character Education in UK Schools: Research Report*, p. 5

12 James Arthur, 2010, *Citizens of Character: New Directions in Character and Values Education*, Exeter: Imprint Academic/Andrews UK Ltd, p. 35.
13 Arthur, *Citizens of Character: New Directions in Character and Values Education*, p. 35.
14 Arthur, *Citizens of Character: New Directions in Character and Values Education*, p. 36.
15 Arthur, *Citizens of Character: New Directions in Character and Values Education*, p. 38.
16 Jean Porter, 2012, 'Virtue Ethics' in Robin Gill (ed.), *The Cambridge Companion to Christian Ethics*, Cambridge: Cambridge University Press, pp. 87–102, p. 87.
17 Daniel C. Russell (ed.), 2013, *The Cambridge Companion to Virtue Ethics*, Cambridge: Cambridge University Press, p. 4.
18 Russell, *The Cambridge Companion to Virtue Ethics*, p. 7.
19 Arthur, *Citizens of Character: New Directions in Character and Values Education*, p. 32.
20 David Brooks, 2015, *The Road to Character*, New York: Penguin Random House, p. ix.
21 Porter, 'Virtue Ethics', p. 90.
22 Porter, 'Virtue Ethics', p. 91.
23 Martin E. P. Seligman, 2002, *Authentic happiness: Using the new positive psychology to realize your potential for lasting fulfilment*, New York, NY: Free Press.
24 Daniel Goleman, 1998, *Working with Emotional Intelligence*, London: Bloomsbury.
25 Agnieszka Bates, 2019, 'Character education and the "priority of recognition"', *Cambridge Journal of Education*, 49(6), pp. 695–710, p. 706.

INTERVIEW WITH
MS CAROLINE BRAGGS,
RETIRED HEADMISTRESS

20 September 2020

CB: I don't know how much you know about Gumley [House], but Gumley is a religious order school. We have two schools in London, two in Liverpool and we've got a school in Jersey. There is an educational trust set up that actually manages that with Sister Brenda, who oversees things. She is now trying to get religious order schools together, so that we are a voice. Because as a body, Catholic religious order schools only come to about 1 per cent of all the schools in the country. Individually, we don't have much of a voice but, if we come together, we would have.

If you go on to the website, our values and our Faithful Companions of Jesus (FCJ) ethos is very much a whole-person education.

MIB: Yes, I noticed that.

CB: So, all the things that you're talking about in your book, we actively, if you like, make sure that equality is there. For instance, if you take languages, we teach French, Spanish, Chinese, Italian and Latin (for high fliers). There is no set scene about whether, you know, you need to do this or you need to do that for a language. If you want to try and do it, you do it. Obviously, there are certain levels, as a linguist yourself, that you might not be able to manage. But if you really wanted to

INTERVIEW

do a French GCSE, we would provide it for you. Our philosophy has never been necessarily just based on ability. I mean something like Chinese, is something that you might say was for the high fliers. But if somebody had a real passion for it, then they would be allowed to do it. And the same, say with the literacy and the language. Now, girls are different [and] people say, 'Oh girls like to read'. They don't actually, after about Year 8 (aged 12/13), very few of them continue reading. So you try and encourage them through novels and things like that. And in a sense, because we are part of a bigger group than just government and education in this country, we come to it from a different way.

MIB: Yes.

CB: When we approach education, we do it where we know there is inequality. We know we are addressing the gaps between this group and this group of students and we balance it out, or try to with the limited funds that we have. When you talk about things like underachievement or inequalities, it is not always necessarily the people [students]. A premium student has that inequality, or the SEN student could actually be the child that is just below the threshold where money is, you know, there is enough to survive on but not enough for the extras.

MIB: I mean it's really interesting that you talk about the religious organization behind it [your former school] because I am a convent girl. I went to the Convent of Jesus and Mary [in Harlesden] and, at that time, we were told that we were part of something bigger, you know, set up by Claudine Thevenet, and all of that. All our year groups were named after saints or prominent religious leaders. So I was [in] Augustine, year 7, 8, 9, 10 and 11. Augustine always were in competition with Genevieve. And it gave us a sense that there was a rooting and rootedness beyond the curriculum, that it was who we were going to be as girls, and how our sense of faith was going to shape who we were as women.

CB: Absolutely, and that I think is why we are different, because it comes from that inner, sort of, belief in something better, and empowering that young woman to take her place, no matter what background she came from, because Gumley isn't purely Catholic; 13 per cent of the students at Gumley came from other faiths. And they enriched our faith and community, with faiths or no faith. It never was an issue whether they were part of the community or not. We never had a division on any front, and we would strive to see where you needed to put the extra funding in, and it's not perhaps where the obvious [gap] would be ... So, from our perspective, I think that because of that faith, we never played the government game. We are not an outstanding school, we are a good school. We'd never be outstanding because I think we'd sell our souls in order to be outstanding.

MIB: That is very powerful.

CB: We would be measured by somebody else's sense of what whole-person education is about.

MIB: What do you think whole-person education is about?

CB: If I could go back to Ignatian tradition: its reflection, its thinking, its action. Or the other way round. Whole person education is not just what goes on literally in the classroom. It's everything. It's all those areas that you're talking about, but also beyond it. It starts from the home, it's your whole being all the time, every action that you're doing. If it is Ignatian, it is going to look around from the world that you're in. And then you're going to reflect on it, you're going to search for meaning, and you're going to act on it. It is not about just simply going through the motions of learn this, do the test, get the grade. And you are not judged, you're not defined by a set of results.

MIB: By the outputs.

INTERVIEW

CB: You're much more than that. You're much more than a set of results. And I don't know about you, but if I went on my O level results and my A level results, I would never have been Head of a school. I wasn't that brilliant!

MIB: Well, I was expelled! So that is a whole different story, Caroline! I mean for me as a Benedictine, it is very much about [this] – I really appreciate Ignatian spirituality because it draws me out of my rhythm of prayer and the sense of balance and grounding and stability that for me – being a Benedictine inculcates in my way of life. I think [though] it is really interesting what you said there about trying to develop this practice in young people and getting them to reflect. Do you think that the way that the state education system has been presented to educators, that it gives room for that level of engagement?

CB: It doesn't and therefore that's why you as an educator have to put that in. For instance, we haven't compromised in Gumley for the arts. We still do drama, music, PE, art. You will still have an hour of that on the curriculum. You will still do performance and production. We don't say to year 11s, 'Oh you can't take art and production, you should be revising for this or that, or that it's only for year 7s' ... You don't put people in boxes. Say something like science, you know, whether you do the triple, as in the three separate sciences, or you do the joint award (it's called something else now), it doesn't matter. You can go on and do the A level in it. Who is to say at 16 you have reached your potential? You may not have. You know, it's not defined by numbers or dates or this linear structure of learning. It is much more about you as a human being. If education isn't about making you fully human, then what is it about?

MIB: This is very powerful.

CB: It's got to be that you are going to change the world.

MIB: That is my view of education. That everybody has the calling on their lives to make the world a better place. At the same time there is a consciousness that perhaps the system doesn't necessarily allow people to feel their sense of purpose. Because it is narrowed down to these outputs.

CB: If you look at the negatives, to actually say that you have a set of subjects that define what's core and what isn't, already you're on to a loser. Because everyone puts the energy into the core, because you exclude all the performance and all your sports and whatever. If you look at the way money is directed, it is directed into sciences and maths. If you're a poet or if you're a musician, or if you're a girl or boy who has got talents in other things, where is that going to be challenged unless the school makes a conscious decision to say that 'we will do this, we will put that on for you'. You talked about trips. We always subsidised our trips so that there was never a child that couldn't go on a trip. When we ran our trips, we actually did a financial four-year plan and put everything out to parents so that they could see, 'Oh, this is coming up'. If you've got more than one child, you can't send one child, say to Iceland, and then somebody else doesn't get to go then. Some people haven't got the money for that [to send all their children on school trips]. And when we did do trips, we gave parents enough time to save. So, you could put in £20 a week or £10 and, if you couldn't, then there were ways of also subsidizing that, so fund it in some sort of way through a school fund. I am not saying that every school could afford to do that. As a church school and a Catholic school, we could do that as a parental contribution. We had funding to help us with that. And I think, it's like with everything, I think education in this country is led by government and it shouldn't be.

MIB: Who should education be led by?

CB: It should be led by practitioners and it should be led by the best educationalists nationally or internationally ... You know

INTERVIEW

when you get a visionary, a visionary education person leading it. And you have a body, you don't just have one person. And you get people from other countries to come and sit on your board and they dictate what the curriculum should be. Ignatius – I mean how long did it take for him to come up with his curriculum – was it about 40 years? So how can you then in this country, have a curriculum that changes every two years, or every year? How can the syllabus that you've taught last year, be out of date this year?

MIB: There is too much tinkering.

CB: And, therefore, if a teacher isn't confident, because you're going into a profession that is a passion, you believe in it, and it keeps changing, you're going to get confused let alone the young person trying to learn from you. I think it is that whole person. I think we don't give enough time for that. We don't give enough time for reflection. Call it what you like, whether it's meditation, whether it's prayer, whether its mindfulness, you know, that moment to sit and think, to be. We don't build it into our curriculum. We have prayer, we have assembly, it's very structured. You don't have that moment in your day where it's just stillness. Where is the stillness in your day to reflect?

MIB: Where do you think the greatest inequalities lie in our education system? This could be as broad or as narrow as you like.

CB: I think it's still to do with funding. I still think it's a money issue, that we are expecting schools to perform on a shoestring. And if you look at budgets, most of the money goes on staffing. A very small percentage actually goes on curriculum and on the needs of the students, and there is nothing you can do about that as a head. That is just what you've got to do. I think we've got to do more. We also don't have the notion of all-round 24-hour education (education that goes beyond the classroom). So, we work on these unreal term times. And the only difference between a middle-class student and a working-class student is one will have parents who will take them on holiday, and show them museums and will do this, that and the other, and the other [student] will not. The brightness of this child and the academic ability of the child are there, it's innate. But the difference is what do you do with them during these holiday times. We don't provide enough. We don't have enough provision for our young people ... I think there is a lot of inequality still where people just label kids. If you come from a certain community, you must be like this. If you come from this community, you must be like that. And I'd say you still get that racist kind of mentality where there is, and it could be for whoever the newest ethnicity is on the block ... We don't actually do the catch-up very well at all. And I think it just gets worse as you go through [the education system]. Although they pump all the money with pupil premium, and they pump all the money in with top ups and all sorts of things, they don't address the actual need. They don't really hear what people are saying. What does that child do when they leave school [each day]? If you look at the hours, you spend actually very few hours in school. Most of this time is spent at home. So constructively what is going on there? ... And if you look at things like poverty levels, I mean the whole introduction of things like, when they took away benefits and brought in Universal Credit, that has just made the rich and poor divide grow. And I had parents who were working two jobs and couldn't afford to keep things going. And I think that in the last two years I gave out more (supermarket) vouchers to parents than I would ever have imagined I would have to do. Something is going wrong, and I don't think it's just, I think education is a symptom of its society.

MIB: That's a lovely phrase.

CB: You know, somebody has said it, it's not me: you judge a society by how you treat your vulnerable, or your children and your elderly, and look at how we're treating all those groups? It's appalling really. If you don't put the money in, you reap what you sow. The only thing I think is still in favour of Britain is its free education, to a certain extent. The minute that goes, we're going to go into Dickens' sort of age. But we still have that notion of children should be in school learning, even if it's a rigid, rote-learning, pass-exams curriculum, they [the children] will have to be there. I don't know how long that is going to last for.

MIB: What would an education system look like that promoted flourishing?

CB: I think you start from the young people from where they're at. You put the funding into the whole person curriculum. So, there's an even divide of your subjects and you get the notion that learning begins at any time and wherever you are, whatever you're doing. And you trust them. You don't have notions like 'no mobile phones', or 'no technology'. Don't be so blinkered. They are using it. They'll just use it behind your back. Teach them how to use it and use it well. And keep them safe. Basically, a school should be a learning, safe environment. Make your mistakes there, so you can flourish. And so, when you leave, you've learned your mistake, and you don't repeat it, if you like. I think you need the funding. You need properly qualified teachers ... When you look at the profession, they leave after four years. They can't take the stress, of the marking, of the paperwork, because the love of learning is not there. It's form filling. It's accountability. It's gone so much the other end, that you think, 'I don't want to do this anymore. I look at my friends doing this [another] job, and they have a life. I don't'. A flourishing school would be that you are accepted the way you are, but you are given the tools, you're given the equipment, you're given the resources to achieve your dreams. There are no ceilings. [If] you want to be a pilot, we'll help you be a pilot. You want to be a ballerina, that's what's going to happen then. And so, the curriculum is formed to help you be the best that you can be. Whatever that might be ... I was probably one of the few Heads that kept their mouths shut when people went on the global climate change march. I know it was the Friday before half term. Of course, they were all off for it. If it had been the Tuesday, I don't know whether they would have gone ... If young people don't have the time to express themselves, what are you going to [do]? I could have just gone down the line. You know, I didn't say yes, I didn't say no ... But there is a part of me that was proud of them, because I thought, 'You know what, you believed in this. You stood up and went on it.' Just like I got emails from the girls who went on the Black Lives Matter march, not because they were trying to be awkward or difficult, [but because] it mattered to them. Had I been young, fitter, I might have gone with them ... So when you say what would an education system look like, that's flourishing, that's what it would look like. Your young people are able to articulate themselves, they're empowered to stand up for the vulnerable, for the needy, for the homeless, whoever [or whatever] they are passionate about, the environment. They have a sense of justice. They have a zest for life, but they also know that it is about service to others. It's not about exploiting somebody. Don't use your brain to hurt other people. It is about being just, it's about service, it's about thinking about people other than yourself. It's about doing something about it. Don't just have the rhetoric, put it into action.

MIB: You're absolutely right. For me, education is telling young people that they are already whole. And that education is not about them proving that they are clever, good or worthy enough. But about society preparing them to engage, and to be active citizens in building social equity and in holding their responsibility for democracy.

CB: People think being gentle is a weak option. No, it isn't. Because to be gentle means that you have that conviction, that strength within to stand up, but do it in a way that doesn't cause offence ... that effects change properly and that you are listened to, basically. That to me is education. It's about making people whole. And if they don't feel whole, because I do think that we are in a broken world actually, people are broken and they are searching, and I think young people are searching, but if you're not careful they will fill that gap in their lives [with] ... the wrong things.

MIB: And poor mentors.

CB: Yes. And if you fill it with faith or spirituality or being or purpose and see outside yourselves ... And people also forget that young people have adolescence right up until the age of 28. It's not this magical school age of between 12 and 16. They are young and they still make mistakes, but we expect them to be adult very, very quickly.

MIB: We do, and I think there is something also about, I was saying to friends, that when I was young, all my mistakes weren't recorded.

CB: And that's what I say to the girls. You know, it's not about, you're not defined by your mistakes. You are not your mistakes. Let them go and learn to forgive yourself.

MIB: Which is very hard for women and especially for young girls.

CB: Girls want to be perfect. If they are not perfect, then they don't feel worthy. It's this cycle 'I am not good enough. I can't do it.' And then it carries on like that, doesn't it?

MIB: It does. I wonder whether now that you are out of it, whether you had any reflections on what would have empowered you, and made your job easier, as a leader in education, not just as a teacher, but as somebody leading teams and budgets and the whole school vision.

CB: I think I was lucky. I had a set of, if you like, Faithful Companions of Jesus (FCJ) Heads with me. If there was a problem, you had a group of headteachers ... not that Hounslow Heads weren't great, they were brilliant too. But because they [FCJ Heads] understood the Catholic nature of what you were trying to do as well ... We have an educational trust officer, Sister Brenda. So, if in doubt, you have this whole order behind you going 'You're doing a grand job. You're really needed. Thank you for the service that you have done.' I don't know how many headteachers get that. To be thanked, to be told you're all right, you're doing OK. There's a support here. If you're having a problem, give us a call. Don't worry about that. And prayer. You know, you wake up in the morning and you pray, and you go to bed and you pray and you know sometimes you just have to say, 'I can't do any more', offer it to the Holy Spirit and ask for help. But it takes quite a person of faith to be able to really do that, and not feel guilty for doing that, and not feel that you're letting someone down by doing that. I would say, what would people need? They [educators] need to have mentors that are meaningful. Not mentors who, because I think a lot of mentors, want you to be like them.

MIB: Yes, mini-mes.

CB: [Yes] because all they want to do is solve a problem for you. They don't actually coach you and they don't help you grow. I am a different Head to what you would be. And so let me be the Head in my style, so I can flourish and I can grow. Because I think [that] unless you're a particular type of Head ... you weren't considered to be a proper Head. Because a proper Head would do this, this, this and this. And would behave in this, this and this [way]. If I look back at what support I needed, I had the support. What I could without was interference from government. But you can't say that can you?

MIB: Yes, you can.

INTERVIEW

CB: If they kept their sticky beaks out of my business, life would have been a lot easier ... If they just kept out of it, stopped interfering, stopped changing things every five minutes, stopped creating the problems. I mean you saw the fiasco through Covid-19 and all the changes that came through every two minutes. And then the results were shocking. If I was a young person, that was so demoralizing. It was degrading for them: 'Oh you didn't get the grade. Now you did get the grade.' So it doesn't mean anything.

MIB: And it really just brought up the argument about testing. Is this really how we are judging our young people, with algorithms, saying that they have passed an exam or failed an exam they never even took?

CB: And part-basing it on historical data from two years' previously. [These kids] had nothing to do with the years before. You should be judged on your own merits, on what you've done. Trust the teachers to have done it right, but we couldn't. I think what were actually doing at the moment is that we're not educating children we're programming them. I did read that so don't think that's me. Somebody said that somewhere, and I thought, 'He's right'. We are not educating, we are programming them for a world that says this, this and this matters.

MIB: Which is not really in line with made in the image of God.

CB: No, not at all.

MIB: With all that potential and all that authority, and all that gifting of stewardship. It's not in there, if we are programming our young people. Because the journey of life is to go back to the centre of love. And if we're not saying that actually this is a journey in which you have to engage through reflection and pause, and action, so that you can go back to the centre of love, the origins of your being, and enable others to do the same, then I think it's a deficit model.

CB: It is a deficit model, absolutely. And for schools that try to do that, you will not get the labels that other schools get. So, we won't be outstanding, and I don't want us to be. You know, you then have to consciously think, 'right, I want to strive to be outstanding, but on my terms not yours'.

MIB: With different criteria.

CB: Yes, because outstanding on whose terms. Who's judging this?

MIB: I just have two more questions that have come to mind based on what we were saying. The first is about mental health and how you feel it is enabled or hindered in the current system.

CB: It is completely and utterly hindered. There is no money for it. I made a conscious decision, but I did it because of historical provision that was put in place. When Sister Brenda was Head of Governors, she brought in counselling. We had counsellors before schools had counsellors. But we had our own counsellors. People had counsellors coming in, but they were buying them in from external providers. So say like the Catholic Society would send counsellors in, but you wouldn't know who you would get. They could change from year to year. There was no consistency, basically, from what you brought in from external services, from the local authority. And she saw that [counselling] as important, but wanted to have someone on site, rather than just have random people come in. So we did have counselling. She also employed a full-time careers officer. We had one 20–25 years ago before it became the norm. And a work experience coordinator. We didn't rely on anyone. When I took over, there was more money then. There is no money now, there is absolutely nothing for pastoral provision at all. Anything you put in is additional money that you have to find from somewhere ... [There] was a conscious decision to put that amount of time into pastoral and mental health provision. And so our PSHE (Personal, Social, Health and Economic) programme covers things like mindfulness, Friends for Life programme. We look at mental health issues, eating disorders. [One of our counsellors] has been great at running parental programming for us as well, helping with workshops, peer training as well. There's nothing [available from government]. If the school doesn't put it in, it won't happen. And we have actually tried to make it part of the curriculum. We talk about things like fears, depression, anxiety, eating disorders, you know, things that actually, I mean because we're a girls school, it would have been very focused on the issues girls would have needed ... And then it would be things like relationships. And then areas also like CSE (child sexual exploitation).

MIB: You were focusing on the body as well as the mind.

CB: And then providing counselling. So different levels depending on what they [students] needed. So even if I take the year 7 programme, Friends for Life, we did the red, amber, green. The red needed the counselling or the really big sort of sessions. The smaller ones did something with our pastoral managers and then others were fine. And it could just well be that transition from year 6 to year 7. And they were fine when they got to year 8. And then in year 8 they had mindfulness, so they actually had the sessions on how to actually just be still, reflect, think, be aware of your surroundings, be aware of what you're doing. How you eat, how you sit, how you sleep. And then self-image was very much part of year 9 work. So, all the way through there would be a particular thing that you would cover. And then also sexuality – a key thing that we have to address. Not have to, we wanted to do it. And I think that when girls did come out and say things like they were transgender or lesbian or something like that, it was treated in a human way, and not something that they felt that they couldn't say to us. So, we didn't have the huge issues. You know some schools hit the press with it because [of the way] it was handled, and letters that went home. You know, we never did the big global thing. It was all done with the parents, with the student, with the people that mattered. And we walk alongside them. Because we don't pretend to know everything, but you learn as you go along. But no, that [mental health provision] is seriously, seriously lacking. When we used to try and do referrals to CAMHS (the NHS's Child and Adolescent Mental Health Services), we learned the tricks from the counsellors. The counsellors ... taught the pastoral managers really what to say and what to do. It's like coded words, isn't it? If you do this, this and this, you're likely to go to the top of the list. And I am sorry to say that maybe we did jump the list. But if that's what my team had to do, they did it, to ensure that our students got what they needed to get. But that funding came from the school, nothing came from government.

MIB: So, the lack of funding to schools is mirrored by the lack of societal provision for the referral process to go through in a way that was holistic for the young person.

CB: Yes ... you have provision and then they cut the provision. This is an external provision. We would have paid for it, but it's not there. So how are we supposed to access something for young people. If you look at what is available to young people, unless you are rich, and that's the only way that I can describe it, you can't do it any other way unless it's private. If CAMHS doesn't take you, you have to go private. And it is very, very limited. It is the wealthy that can afford the Priory fees or wherever else you decide to take your child. And it looks like more and more girls are getting into that sort of, when they hit 15 or 16, that whole issue of serious mental health where they get hospitalized.

MIB: Is there an argument for reviewing the way we set out the academic year?

INTERVIEW

CB: Yes. I don't know what makes 39 weeks magical. But there you go ... In the north, they used to go back slightly differently in August, because they were farming communities there. They would go in earlier, because then they were needed for the harvest. So they adapted it [the system] to suit that community's need. Surely isn't that what we should be doing wherever we are? And six weeks in the summer sometimes is just too long a time for some of our young people if they are just in London wandering the streets.

MIB: Because the youth clubs have also been closed.

CB: If you're living on estates, some of which are dangerous places, why would you want six weeks of hanging around there? It would be much better, if we did things like, six weeks, two weeks' break, six weeks, two weeks' break. Or you do the semesters like the Americans and Europeans, where there is a chunk of time, you get your seasonal and religious festivals within that time. You're constantly doing it in chunks as opposed to bizarre timings. Like the spring term. Sometimes you can have a four week [half] term and then an eight week [half] term, because of where Easter falls. And it does not make sense at all. I think the whole review of that would be important, because I think that's where the uneven divide [is] – it would help those children who don't have activities to do during the holidays. And you run activities through the holiday for them. If you're sitting around at home doing nothing, why not go into school and do some art work or have something like a youth club where, all right it's not school, but run it like a youth club. So, you go on day trips, you go to the museum and you go to the seaside, you go into central London.

MIB: I remember I was living north of the river and I was teaching. My first teaching job was at a sixth form college in south London, and some of my boys said, 'Yeah Miss where do you live?' And I said, 'Well north of the river'. And they were shocked because they had never crossed the river.

INEQUALITY AND FLOURISHING

CB: And why would you, because you just stay in your little area.

MIB: Yes, exactly ... There is so much potential isn't there?

CB: There is ... [In] *Outliers* by Malcolm Gladwell, I think he hit it on the nail that the difference ... is opportunity. It's the opportunity and life chances [that make a difference].

Period 2: English and Modern Languages

Language and Liberation

When the day of Pentecost had come, they were all together in one place. And suddenly from heaven there came a sound like the rush of a violent wind, and it filled the entire house where they were sitting. Divided tongues, as of fire, appeared among them, and a tongue rested on each of them. All of them were filled with the Holy Spirit and began to speak in other languages, as the Spirit gave them ability.

Now there were devout Jews from every nation under heaven living in Jerusalem. And at this sound the crowd gathered and was bewildered, because each one heard them speaking in the native language of each. Amazed and astonished, they asked, 'Are not all these who are speaking Galileans? And how is it that we hear, each of us, in our own native language? Parthians, Medes, Elamites, and residents of Mesopotamia, Judea and Cappadocia, Pontus and Asia, Phrygia and Pamphylia, Egypt and the parts of Libya belonging to Cyrene, and visitors from Rome, both Jews and proselytes, Cretans and Arabs – in our own languages we hear them speaking about God's deeds of power.' All were amazed and perplexed, saying to one another, 'What does this mean?' But others sneered and said, 'They are filled with new wine.'
(Acts 2.1–13)

There is something about being understood that affirms our human dignity. That someone speaks our language, that someone hears us, and can connect with us, helps to break down barriers and facilitates new relationships. The Holy Spirit is linked to a plurality of expression that meets people where they are. It cleaves to the authentic and seeks to transform for the purpose of welcome. In doing so our own gifts are enriched and deepened.

The Holy Spirit does not segregate us according to human divisions, but rather is a gatherer of people and a disrupter of barriers. Each human being has the potential for a Spirit-filled encounter with the divine, in which God removes human impossibility and returns to the notion of 'what if?' The Holy Spirit fills the space and leaves a legacy for the common good. There is a sense of deep and broad hospitality that recognizes all, and gives room for different voices and accents, and opportunities to engage. The Holy Spirit creates a noise for action, a noise for positive social change.

In speaking the other languages of those present, the possibility of hearing and telling a new story was opened. People, not already in the narrative, could be brought in. Other tongues would bring new perspectives and new journeys that celebrate rather than undermine the different points of departure. The languages heard spoke to the origins of the listeners, but also spoke of the future and their role in it. Languages give both the speaker and the listener the opportunity to co-create and construct new meaning through familiar and unfamiliar words. There is a new freedom to express connection and purpose without fear of being misunderstood.

There is no doubt that this invitation of the Holy Spirit is filled with risk and vulnerability. In speaking a language that is not necessarily our own we are left exposed to ridicule, and to shame, to explain what you thought was obvious and clear. There is this temporary waiting room before flourishing and before deeper forms of expression. Our hellos can be multiplied, and our goodbyes held. To enter into this space and to offer yourself to new learning and new understanding opens horizons of possibility, and the realization that our world is bigger than ourselves alone. Our view and definitions do not speak or represent other communities and ways of living. Our corpus is not the be all and end all of human endeavour or

PERIOD 2: ENGLISH AND MODERN LANGUAGES

expression. Language learning resists a limited worldview and challenges us to step into the shoes of others, and to be prepared to be amazed at what we see, and what we learn, and how this can change our entire lives.

* * *

Perhaps the firm and constant presence of *Junior English Revised* by Haydn Richards[1] was the symbol and chronicle of a life foretold. The crumpled 42nd impression published in 1991 testifies to the place this book has had in my life. The book, with its creased cover and spine, has been packed into multiple suitcases and boxes and has travelled across continents. This book, which I have had since I was a little girl, speaks of the importance language and languages would hold in my life as both a learner and a teacher. I absolutely loved reading the chapters and working through the exercises. From St Saviour's primary school in Lagos to St Mary's C of E primary school, Willesden, the boasted dual aim of the book 'to teach and to test English' has come to signify more than simply being able to speak and read and write. It has been a book about how language places you and shapes the world around you, and facilitates cultural, intellectual and emotional expression.

My experience of schooling was mixed. I always enjoyed learning and school seemed to allow for that at a younger age. Born in London, I had some primary education in Lagos, Nigeria, and some in London where my family finally settled in the early 1990s. I had a double promotion in Lagos from Year 4 to Year 6 because the teachers felt that I could cope, and that Year 5 would have been a waste of time for a learner like me. I repeated part of Year 6 when we moved to London so I could start secondary school at aged 11, which was thought best for me at the time. My secondary school experience was shaped by the belief that girls were just as intelligent, capable and competitive as boys. The Convent of Jesus and Mary Language College which provided my Catholic girls school education was to thank for that. And for my intense dislike of tights.

At school, I excelled and fell in love with learning languages. All my languages teachers had a connection to the Republic of Ireland. I grew up thinking that everyone in Ireland must have been a gifted polyglot who woke up each day speaking multiple languages. This love propelled me to study languages to PhD level and to teach Spanish at secondary level. I gained a place on the Postgraduate Certificate of Education course (training to become a qualified teacher) at the University of Cambridge, while finishing my PhD, but decided to complete my doctorate first instead of pausing it.

Modern Foreign Languages

The study and teaching of Modern Foreign Languages (MFL) in English state secondary schools has waxed and waned since the 1970s. There was the issue of the system itself not being conducive to the successful promoting of MFL:

> Under the selective system of 'grammar' and 'secondary modern' schools which dominated English state secondary education until the mid-1970s, most pupils in the latter did not study MFL, yet they comprised over 80% of the school population. Teaching MFL to pupils of all abilities in the recently introduced comprehensive schools was thus a new experience for language teachers, nearly all of whom had learned their trade in grammar schools. Furthermore, before 1986, teachers often had to prepare pupils in the same class for two different examinations: General Certificate of Education (GCE) O-level and the Certificate of Secondary Education (CSE). These examinations had different syllabuses and grading systems and were targeted at different ranges of ability. Since the former prioritised translation and the latter listening and speaking, this presented a daunting challenge.[2]

PERIOD 2: ENGLISH AND MODERN LANGUAGES

The introduction of the National Curriculum in the 1980s allowed teachers to start to think of the place of languages as part of the core educational provision for learners. Further, the work being done beyond the UK within the Council of Europe (COE)[3] meant that there was external support for pedagogical thinking, and a focus on best practice, curriculum design and development:

> Meanwhile, between 1982 and 1987, extensive work on MFL curricula and methodology involving 15 countries was being undertaken by the COE Project No. 12 'Learning and Teaching Modern Languages for Communication' (COE 1988). This project led to a consensus in Europe on the importance of international communication as a basic aim of modern language teaching and identified priorities for further work on language learning and teaching methodology and the training of language teachers. The COE work had a considerable influence on the National Curriculum MFL Working Group (MFLWG) (1989-1990) set up by the DES and chaired by Professor Martin Harris; MFLWG subsequently proposed MFL for all for the new National Curriculum to operate from 1992.[4]

The result of all this work is that the 'first version of the National Curriculum for MFL was published in 1991'.[5] The curriculum would have clear aims and there would be allocated time per week for the teaching of MFL in schools. The curriculum aimed to be 'accessible to all pupils, with a communicative approach, reflected in a Programme of Study (PoS) which would present pupils with a more challenging experience of MFL up to the age of 16'.[6]

There would, however, be a review of the National Curriculum in 1993, just two years after the first version of the National Curriculum for MFL was published. There had been hardly any time for the curriculum to be embedded and the 'main remit of Sir Ron Dearing's review[7] was to slim down the curriculum'.[8] Yet, it is important to note that 'significant progress was made after MFL in Key Stage 4 (KS4 is ages 14–16) became compulsory in 1996. By 2000 around 90% of pupils were taking an MFL and 79% were entered for GCSE'.[9] A key publication in 2000 by the Nuffield Foundation offered ways to promote and embed language learning:

> The Nuffield Inquiry (The Nuffield Foundation 2000) produced recommendations covering all aspects of language learning at all stages. The National Strategy for Languages for England (DfES 2002) adopted many of the Nuffield recommendations including the appointment of a National Director for Languages in 2003. A range of centrally funded initiatives followed. These included:
> - the 'Framework for Languages' at KS3 produced by the Department for Children, Schools and Families setting out a structured and progressive set of teaching objectives for MFL, based on good practice, to support teachers in their planning[10] (Evans and Fisher 2009: 1).
> - the 'Asset Languages' scheme which offered students an alternative route to GCSE and access to a qualification in a wide range of languages for which GCSE was not available (see ALL 2012).
> - the national 'Links into Languages' programme which provided regional hubs, access to specialists of national standing and a bank of materials for the targeted professional development of language teachers.[11]

The initiatives that stemmed from the Nuffield Inquiry focused on both how to support teachers and students across different educational pathways and at different stages of school.

There was also growing momentum to offer sustained support to teachers who:

> ... benefitted from a strong infrastructure involving the network of specialist Language Colleges, first established in 1995, and the internationally respected Centre for Information on Language Teaching and Research (CILT), founded

in 1966, which offered a ready-made platform for teacher and materials development and a unique specialist library resource. In common with their colleagues in other subjects, MFL teachers also had access to information, advice and training via the Qualifications and Curriculum Development Agency (QCDA) and the Training and Development Agency for Schools (TDA).[12]

The reality is that this decade needs to be seen as one of addition and subtraction to MFL provision in schools by successive governments. On the one hand we have recommendations, and the framework of professional support for MFL teachers. On the other, you have another policy change a few years later that would have long-lasting ramifications for both teachers and learners:

> ... this progress was undermined in 2003 when the then Secretary of State for Education, seeking more flexibility in the KS4 curriculum, decided that MFL should no longer be compulsory after age 14 from 2004 onwards.[13]

This was a major shake-up, but it is not as first thought. The idea that languages were no longer obligatory seems to put the emphasis on the child or young person deciding they could 'drop' the language they found annoying or difficult, and finally breathe a sigh of relief that they were no longer in that particular class. The reality is that the student was not the focal point of this policy change at all:

> In 2004, the government did not 'make languages optional', as is sometimes claimed; it allowed schools to do so as part of the strategy of granting them greater autonomy. At the same time, it demanded more accountability from schools for 'delivering' successful outcomes for pupils, and it did so through the examination system. This meant that not only were schools responsible for deciding which subjects beyond the core should remain compulsory, if any, but that they

could manipulate the ways that options were presented to pupils in order to achieve the most beneficial outcomes in school league tables. With languages regarded by pupils and curriculum managers alike as a 'difficult' subject, the only way was down for numbers studying the subject.[14]

Therefore, MFL became a political pawn in the wider policy shifts that were occurring from 2000 onwards. The consequences of removing MFL from the core subjects offered in a school have indirectly and directly shaped the way society views languages in schools. What we also see with the Conservative–Liberal Democrat Coalition Government (2010–15) is a deconstruction of the previous investment in MFL and an intentional diminution of its status and importance in schools:

> The new policy was one of minimal intervention and the infrastructure outlined above was broken up. The National Centre for Languages (CILT) and the Qualifications and Curriculum Development Agency (QCDA) were closed down. The Training and Development Agency for Schools (TDA) was replaced with the Teaching Agency, which subsequently merged with the National College for School Leadership. The Specialist Schools programme, the National Strategy, 'Links into Languages' and Asset Languages were all discontinued. The post of National Director for Languages was abolished in 2011. Funding previously earmarked specifically for languages was transferred to general school budgets. The still valuable materials produced under publicly funded initiatives, such as 'Links into Languages', are now only available for those teachers who know where to look on the National Archives website.[15]

Thus, by the time the UK European membership referendum of 23 June 2016 took place, the scene had already been set. The UK was now faced with the reality of not having the adequate infrastructure to support teachers of MFL, not promoting or safeguarding the place of MFL in the curriculum and not being

PERIOD 2: ENGLISH AND MODERN LANGUAGES

part of a transnational political and educational community that invested in and encouraged language learning.

To view MFL as unimportant in schools irrevocably breaks the talent pipeline of potential linguists for universities and future workplaces:

> Crucially for the supply of linguists, A-level entries for languages have also declined: numbers sitting French have dropped by a third and those for German by nearly half since 2002. This in turn has had a baleful impact on university provision for languages at degree level, where there have been widespread closures and shrinkages.[16]

This impact continues to be felt with the almost annual reduction in university languages departments across the UK and the sense that MFL are dispensable at secondary school level. The global pandemic and the resulting changes to the UK assessment at ages 16 (GCSEs) and 18 (A levels) underlined the further decline in language learning. For example, with GCSEs in MFL:

> Entries for all subjects rose by 3%, with entries for French, German, and Spanish combined also rising by 3% – confirmation of the levelling out of previous declines we have seen over the past 3 years or so. Within this group of languages – those most commonly taught in schools – we also see a continuation of the trend towards increasing numbers taking Spanish (+7% this year on 2019). Entries for French increased by 1% and German declined by 1%, both welcome signs given declines of 22% and 29% respectively in these languages over the preceding five years.
>
> Entries for other languages have fared much worse in 2020. As a group, the 'lesser-taught' languages have declined by 28% compared to 2019, after remaining fairly stable over the previous five years. That previous stability among the group as a whole, masked substantial variations between different languages, with Chinese, Arabic, and Polish seeing

healthy increases, while Panjabi, Urdu and Japanese saw declines. Between 2019 and 2020, only Modern Hebrew language saw increased entries. With that exception, there were fewer entries for all the lesser taught languages with declines ranging from -48% for Polish to -10% for Chinese.[17]

The challenge for us all is that it is very easy for language learning to become the preserve of a small section of society, those in schools in which languages are still obligatory, and those with the means to learn languages beyond the school day or walls. We know that 'although the declines in participation in languages beyond the age of 14 have affected all types of school, there is plentiful evidence to show that this is increasingly associated with socio-economic disadvantage, poverty and areas of the country affected by economic decline'.[18] It is easy, therefore, for languages to become the preserve of the economically able and those in schools that have the investment to continue with their MFL offering. As we emerge at the beginning of this new decade, from a pandemic the impact of which will be felt for years, and as a country that is no longer part of the European Union:

> It is even more important that languages are made relevant and accessible for all, not just for an academic elite. The role of schools in promoting openness, tolerance and friendship across borders will become even more critical ... The cultural and intercultural learning which takes place through friendly contact with speakers of other languages benefits all pupils and society at large, and must be given value alongside academic success in language learning as measured through the exams. We may need to find ways other than the current exam system to support, recognise and value this.[19]

PERIOD 2: ENGLISH AND MODERN LANGUAGES

English as an Additional Language

The importance of MFL sits alongside the key considerations about how schools are enabled to support those who have English as an Additional Language (EAL). To be designated as an EAL learner means that you already speak, write or have knowledge of another language. This should be a cause for a celebration, but it is often seen as a problem that needs to be fixed, with a deficit framework used in which it is almost as if it is the child's fault for not having spoken English from the womb. The notion of language as a problem is not new:

> Ruiz[20] proposed three basic perspectives about language around which people and groups vary: *language as a problem, language as right and language as a resource* [emphasis in the original]. These three different dispositions may be conscious, but they are also embedded in the subconscious assumptions of teachers, planners and politicians. Such orientations are regarded as fundamental and related to a basic philosophy or ideology held by an individual or group.[21]

The presentation of language as a problem means that to have a language that is different to the main language of delivery in an educational setting places the student in the position of needing to be 'fixed'. This approach and philosophy are diametrically opposed to child-centred teaching and learning, and to supporting the flourishing of children and young people. Further, students who have EAL are often all grouped together, with policies and educational interventions seeing them as one body of learners. Yet,

> Pupils with English as an additional language are not a homogeneous group. Teachers and educational policy makers need to be aware of the range of variables in relation to both individual learners and groups. These variables will also be significant when interpreting the overall task which learning EAL entails:

- Some pupils are born in the UK but enter school speaking little or no English and have limited or no experience of literacy in their first language.
- Some pupils are born in the UK but enter school speaking little or no English. However, they have some experience of literacy in their first languages.
- Some pupils arrive between the ages of 5 and 16 without literacy or oracy skills in English but with age equivalent skills in literacy and oracy in their first languages, and sometimes in other languages as well.
- Some pupils enter the school system between the ages of 5 and 16 without literacy or oracy skills in English and with limited or no literacy skills in their first language due to disrupted schooling.

In addition, some pupils have suffered emotional and psychological stress as a result of family loss or social and economic disruption to their lives in their countries of origin.[22]

If the aim is flourishing, then the heterogeneity of students who have EAL must be not only recognized but celebrated as the starting point in which the needs of the child or young person are carefully assessed and addressed in a sustained and sustainable way. Speaking a language other than English should not be seen as a barrier to flourishing, but rather as another dimension in which flourishing can take root.

As with MFL teaching, there is also something here about the infrastructure at a national level that enables the support and teaching of EAL in schools. Researchers note that 'the most potentially damaging feature of EAL policy in England is the absence of any national oversight or provision of professional qualifications, staff development and specialist roles for teachers and other school staff working with children with EAL'.[23] It is a bit like being asked to ride a bike with just a wheel, with no frame offered, let alone a saddle.

Unfortunately, the most recent news on government policy relating to EAL emphasizes this lack of care for and attention to EAL students:

PERIOD 2: ENGLISH AND MODERN LANGUAGES

NALDIC has learned that Ofsted is to abolish the role of National Lead for EAL, ESOL and Gypsy, Roma and Travellers. It has done so without consultation and, it appears, without regard for the impact on bilingual children in our schools. Ofsted has, at a stroke, removed much needed official oversight of an important area of our educational provision. The old adage 'out of sight, out of mind' is apt: this retrograde step will undermine our collective efforts to raise attainment among minoritized pupils.

Ofsted is the Office for Standards in Education, Children's Services and Skills. It aspires to be a 'force for improvement through intelligent, responsible and focused inspection' ... Understanding EAL and demanding that schools meet high standards for EAL pupils is therefore a litmus test of the organisation's effectiveness and relevance. By removing the key role of National Lead for EAL, English for speakers of other languages (ESOL) and Gypsy, Roma and Traveller pupils, Ofsted fails that test ...

We see the hard bigotry of no expectations, of pupils whose needs are clearly understood being failed because government departments and the inspectorate no longer think they are worthy of attention.[24]

There has to be a better way than this. The current education system cannot be separate from the society in which it is housed. The sense that any language other than English is not as important permeates the approach to opportunities and access for EAL students. If a child is blessed enough to have had exposure to one, two or even three languages before or alongside English, there should be an education system that can honour that, hold that learning and incorporate that knowledge into a wider framework of language acquisition, promotion and use.

The current predicament, in which MFL has been devalued and having a language that is not English in a child's linguistic repertoire undervalued, means that there is little room to nurture students who have an interest, gifts or skills in languages.

In addition, to have EAL needs to be seen as a resource not as a problem. There needs to be a radical shift in policy and investment to enable children and young people to flourish as language learners, whether or not they have EAL. If students do have EAL, the education system and policies need to move away from blame to affirmation, from othering to inclusivity, from devaluation to the celebration of what other languages bring to educational spaces:

> Cummins[25] suggests that minority language students are *'empowered'* or *'disabled'* by four major characteristics of schools:
>
> 1. The extent to which minority language students' home language and culture are incorporated into the school curriculum.
> 2. The extent to which minority communities are encouraged to participate in their children's education.
> 3. The extent to which education promotes the inner desire for children to become active seekers of knowledge and not just passive receptacles.
> 4. The extent to which the assessment of minority language students avoids locating problems in the student and seeks to find the root of the problem in the social and educational system or curriculum wherever possible.[26]

What we see here is the potential for EAL to become part of a broader and more engaging curriculum in which children and young people become active participants in the learning journey. The education system that has been created is not separate from the wider issues in society. If there is inequality in it, it is because these inequalities are embedded in the construction of our society as it currently stands. The child or young person who brings multiple heritages into the school environment challenges the limited and disempowering culture rooted in archaic models of an education system that does not speak to the future of interdependence and collaboration, which are essential for tackling global and national challenges across communities and nation states. We need an education system that empowers children and young people – and that seems to be what governments and policy makers are afraid of:

> *Empowerment* thus becomes an important concept in transforming the situations of many language minorities. 'Empowerment means the process of acquiring power, or the process of transition from lack of control to the acquisition of control over one's life and immediate environment.'[27] Empowerment means movement for minority language students from coercive, superior–inferior (subordinate) relationships, to collaborative relationships, power sharing and power creating, where identities or minorities are affirmed and voiced.[28]

This movement towards 'power sharing and power creating' does not favour the superior–inferior model in which English is placed at the top and every other language beneath it. To fully provide for and support learners who have EAL is to recognize that our society is made of many peoples and identities and that these different cultures and heritages need space in our education system. This is about richness not a deficit mode, in which all children and young people are given the access to and opportunities for flourishing.

English in secondary schools

The centrality of language, of its relationship with thought, and its role in learning, is fundamental to education.[29] This is the case whether we are learning a language we call our own, English or MFL. We have already explored where and how MFL and EAL sit within the current state secondary system. The final part of this examination into language is necessarily about English itself and how the study of this subject in schools to date has been constructed.

English has been taught in schools since the beginning of the twentieth century:

> Why is the subject called 'English'? While the first university to offer an English degree was Oxford in 1893,[30] it was in 1904 that the Board of Education required subjects of English literature and language to be taught in English schools.[31] This coincided with the further establishment of English as a university subject, partly as a reaction to World War I and partly as a 'civilising'[32] means of social control.[33]

Its introduction into schools and higher education more broadly suggests a deeper relationship with the subject and politics nationally and internationally. To write about English is to enter not only into the political dimension of the language and subject, but to reflect on the impact of the subject and how it is taught and valued in and beyond school. The societal value placed on any subject heightens or decreases its importance within school and in discussions around the curriculum within education policy.

English is linked to empire and that is a fact that needs to be acknowledged and reflected in any curriculum:

> From its outset as a school subject, English has thus been fraught with anxieties about its nature and purpose. Its very name implies an imperialistic attempt to bring together disparate factions under a nationalistic banner – an indication of efforts to define the subject's ontology.[34]

English as a language of empire is not taught as such in schools today. Rather secondary school English is a different thing altogether:

> From the inception of the 1989 National Curriculum, SSE [Secondary School English] has been neatly atomised for planning and assessment purposes into three distinct areas: reading, writing, and speaking and listening, more recently termed 'Spoken Language' (Department for Education, 2013).[35]

The result is a subject that has been shaped by and for assessment. Students are encouraged to build their skills in the aforementioned areas often without interrogating what studying English means and how this is often placed in opposition to the learning of other languages.

Few students' relationship today with SSE would be marked by a textbook, like that of my closeness to the *Junior English Revised* by Haydn Richards, which focused more on the English language and mastering the grammar:

> SSE as it is taught between the ages of eleven to fourteen in secondary schools will incorporate most of the following as topics for teaching:
> - literature (both from the English canon and modern prose and poetry)
> - non-fiction
> - media
> - drama
> - discrete teaching of grammar
> - 'reading' lessons (often held in the library), designed to encourage reading for pleasure.[36]

Looking at this range of topics you would be forgiven for thinking that SSE was a dynamic and plural subject. Yet this also is not as it seems. Texts considered part of the canon can be narrow and may not necessarily celebrate different cultures and heritages. The intervention of Government, once again, in the curriculum led to further narrowing of what could be studied within this subject:

> [During the Coalition Government] there was a particular emphasis on more traditional forms of pedagogy, 'real subjects' and 'facts' – what Michael Gove (Secretary of State for Education 2010–14) called a move away from 'soft' and 'airy fairy' subjects and towards more 'rigour' and 'the best which has been thought and said'. Gove also argued for more 'patriotic history', the restoration of times tables and more work on British authors in English literature courses

– resulting in the dropping of *To Kill a Mockingbird* and *Of Mice and Men* from GCSE English examinations.[37]

Removing American literature from the curriculum speaks to a particular association between English as a subject in schools and a broader nationalistic agenda. What exactly Gove thought reading Harper Lee or John Steinbeck would do to students or their notion of identity remains to be determined. Again, we can see the historic legacy of imperialist thinking: 'our English is better than your English, our ways are better than yours'. This mode of thinking has little to do with learning or placing children and young people at the centre of the education system and its approaches.

We have, therefore, in SSE a rather limited and reductive subject that does not necessarily empower students to celebrate their place within a rich and plural notion of English, or *Englishes*:

> Perhaps more indicative of the state's view of SSE is in what is absent, rather than what is explicitly mentioned in the National Curriculum. There is no reference to creativity in the current version; a sharp difference to the previous National Curriculum, which had creativity as one of its central tenets (QCA, 2007) and only one reference to 'interpretations' (p. 4) (and this only in relation to staging of plays). Media or multimodal texts are notable omissions; a retrogressive decision as much consumption of texts, particularly by young people, is likely to be in digital format. It seems, therefore, that the 'Cultural Analysis' model of English with a wider definition of 'texts', has less purchase with the current National Curriculum. Spoken language is similarly neglected; despite the admission that spoken language 'continues to underpin the development of pupils' reading and writing',[38] it is relegated to the end of the document. That it is no longer counted as part of the GCSE qualification (taken by most pupils at age sixteen) indicates the lack of importance placed on speaking and listening, belying the earlier statement.[39]

PERIOD 2: ENGLISH AND MODERN LANGUAGES

English as it is presently taught in schools leaves little room for active co-creation between student and subject. We are expected to see SSE as unquestionable, but question it we must. It does not serve our children and young people well, and this is neither their fault nor that of the teachers who love working to excite and inspire their students with this subject. The truth of the matter is that the system has created a subject that has been stripped of its potency to transform world views and enable students to creatively articulate their relationship with language and text.

The primacy of Standard English influenced the setting of standards in England's National Curriculum and continues to influence educational policy to this day.[40] Yet, the promotion of Standard English also has to be interrogated because the notion of 'standard' is assumed and has historical antecedents.

> While the complaint tradition[41] has ensured that 'Standard English' has been held as the ideal model for education since at least the seventeenth century ... this viewpoint was increasingly entrenched in the United Kingdom following the move away from the briefly more pluralistic stances of the 1970s.[42]

In reality, Standard English is a nebulous and abstract concept that may mean little to students and teachers alike. Children and young people need to be encouraged to celebrate their ability to engage with the plurality of language, whether this is beyond or within English itself.

Another option is to decentre Standard English, resituating it as just one of a range of Englishes available, dependent on context.[43] Many teachers are probably already doing this in numerous contexts[44] but it is under-discussed and not officially condoned.[45] This has the potential to be transformative for both teachers and children, as they become critically aware of the linguistic repertoires that they already control and can expand, potentially giving them a sense of power over their own language use and choices. Practically,

Wheeler and Swords[46] discussed using contrastive analysis as one of the most beneficial techniques for both teachers and students in terms of raising awareness of the grammaticality of other varieties, and changing attitudes, with teachers challenged to change their terminology from a deficit, prescriptive approach to a descriptive one that emphasised building on students' linguistic repertoires, rather than replacing the stigmatised variety with the 'standard'.[47]

Being able to reproduce Standard English comes with societal judgement and reward, while being unable is met with stigmatization. This is the direct result of the structures created with SSE and the way the subject has been allowed to be codified within the National Curriculum. Not having Standard English is subtly linked to disadvantage and this means that children and young people are labelled and also judged, once again, within a deficit model

> The current pathologisation and medicalisation of socially disadvantaged children have echoes of the way that learners of English and users of creoles, pidgins, and hybrids have been treated over time.[48] The lack of focus on the root causes of the disadvantage (which is, of course, not linguistic) must, of course, be rectified for any significant improvement to be seen at an educational level by 'shout(ing) louder' about it as Grainger[49] puts it.[50]

It cannot be said enough that the child is never at fault when placed within an education structure and system that reflects and reinforces the disadvantages and inequalities of wider society.

Reimagining language learning

How can we do this better? How can we legitimatize and secure the place of the learning of other languages, the equitable and sustained support of students who have EAL, and a

PERIOD 2: ENGLISH AND MODERN LANGUAGES

more pluralistic approach to English in schools? A key step would be to bring the three elements of the same issue together in one national body. EAL is often classified as 'an additional/ special need' rather than seen as part of a strategy to encourage language learning and acquisition. A national body of this kind would bring together those who have led in this field for decades, for example NALDIC (the national subject association for English as an additional language), together with key associations such as CIOL (Chartered Institute of Linguists) and NATE (the National Association for the Teaching of English), the British Council, alongside classroom teachers, researchers and university lecturers. The aim of this new body would be the creation of a national strategy for languages that was holistic in its approach and which placed the learner at the centre. This strategy would work to realign English alongside the learning of MFL as one of the many languages open to children and young people in order the deconstruct the often-prejudicial hierarchies inherent in the promotion of standard English. This strategy would also look to dismantle the National Curriculum to create a more diverse configuration of subjects around knowledge of languages that sought to empower students to focus on learning and creative engagement with language and text rather than limiting assessment.

At a school level, liberation from the National Curriculum would be supported by specialist training and support around the different languages in communities and the plural heritages that can be celebrated through literature and varied textual and verbal representations. There would also be the opportunity for teachers to develop skills and understanding around second language acquisition, unpicking their biases and working to affirm and reshape their student's relationship with the languages in their lives. The benefits of speaking more than one language would be celebrated as would the opportunities for cultural exchange and learning. There would be designated time in the school day for language learning and support for pre- and post-school engagement with languages. Imagine a day in the week that was dedicated to English alongside Spanish, Urdu and Yoruba, Hebrew, French, Hindi, German, Arabic, Mandarin and Cantonese, with community links and national and international partnerships highlighted and brought into the learning environment. Each week each student would know that language and languages matter, and that languages can foster liberation and empower the spirit, mind and intellect.

Notes

1 Haydn Richards, 1960, reprinted 1991, *Junior English Revised*, Aylesbury: Ginn and Company Ltd.

2 Alan Dobson, 2018, 'Towards "MFL for all" in England: a historical perspective', *The Language Learning Journal*, 46(1), pp. 71–85, pp. 72–3.

3 The European Union and the Council of Europe are frequently confused, not least because the EU adopted the COE's flag and anthem, but they are completely separate organizations. The COE was founded by the Treaty of London in 1949. It now has 47 member states and a total population of over 800 million. Its *raison d'être* is based on the three pillars of democracy, human rights and the rule of law. One of its main initiatives in the 1990s was to provide curricular and teacher education support for the new democracies in Eastern Europe after the break-up of the Soviet Union. The COE works by consensus. Unlike the EU, it does not issue directives, and its recommendations are always qualified by a statement referring to the 'national, regional or local circumstances' of each member state. The European Centre for Modern Languages (ECML) (www.ecml.at) is a COE institution, but member states are not automatically members of the ECML: any of the 47 member states of the COE may opt into membership under an 'Enlarged Partial Agreement'. Before the UK left in 2011, the ECML had 34 member states. The EU (formerly European Economic Community) was founded in 1956 by the Treaty of Rome and adopted its present name in Maastricht in 1993. It has 28 states and a total population of about 500 million. The organization began as an economic union but, particularly since Maastricht, has embraced a wide range of policy areas including environment, health, external relations and security. The EU's budget of over Đ140 billion is many times greater than that of the COE (about Đ450 million) (Dobson, 2018, pp. 82).

4 Dobson, 'Towards "MFL for all" in England: a historical perspective', pp. 72–3.

PERIOD 2: ENGLISH AND MODERN LANGUAGES

5 Dobson, 'Towards "MFL for all" in England: a historical perspective', p. 74.
6 Dobson, 'Towards "MFL for all" in England: a historical perspective', p. 74.
7 UK Government, 1994, *The Dearing Review; The National Curriculum and its Assessment: Final Report*, available from www.educationengland.org.uk/documents/dearing1994/dearing1994.html, accessed 28.02.2022.
8 Dobson, 'Towards "MFL for all" in England: a historical perspective', p. 75.
9 Dobson, 'Towards "MFL for all" in England: a historical perspective', p. 76.
10 Michael Evans and Linda Fisher, 2009, *Language Learning at Key Stage 3*, Research Brief DCSF-RB091, London: DCSF, p. 1.
11 Dobson, 'Towards "MFL for all" in England: a historical perspective', p. 78.
12 Dobson, 'Towards "MFL for all" in England: a historical perspective', p. 78.
13 Dobson, 'Towards "MFL for all" in England: a historical perspective', p. 76.
14 Teresa Tinsley, 2018, 'Languages in English Secondary Schools Post-Brexit' in Michael Kelly (ed.), *Languages after Brexit: How the UK Speaks to the World*, Cham, Switzerland: Palgrave Macmillan, p. 130.
15 Dobson, 'Towards "MFL for all" in England: a historical perspective', p. 78.
16 Tinsley, 'Languages in English Secondary Schools Post-Brexit', p. 127.
17 Teresa Tinsley, 2020, 'Coronavirus and languages GCSEs, 2020', 16 October, *Alcantara Communications*, www.alcantaracoms.com/coronavirus-and-languages-gcses-2020/, accessed 28.02.2022.
18 Tinsley, 'Languages in English Secondary Schools Post-Brexit', pp. 127–8.
19 Tinsley, 'Languages in English Secondary Schools Post-Brexit', pp. 134–5.
20 Richard Ruiz, 1984, 'Orientations in language planning', *NABE Journal*, 8, pp. 15–34.
21 Colin Baker, 2011 (5th edn), *Foundations of Bilingual Education and Bilingualism*, Bristol: Multilingual Matters, p. 375.
22 NALDIC, 'EAL Learners in Schools', *National Subject Association for EAL*, https://naldic.org.uk/the-eal-learner/eal-learners-uk/eal-learners-in-schools/, accessed 28.02.2022.
23 Jo Hutchinson, 2018, 'Educational Outcomes of Children with English as an Additional Language', *The Bell Foundation*, www.bell-

foundation.org.uk/eal-programme/research/educational-outcomes-of-children-with-english-as-an-additional-language/, p. 9, accessed 20.05.2021.

24 EAL Journal, 2021, 'Ofsted removes one of the voices for EAL in the inspectorate', *EAL Journal*, 29 March, https://ealjournal.org/2021/03/29/ofsted-removes-one-of-the-voices-for-eal-in-the-inspectorate/, accessed 28.02.2022.

25 Jim Cummins, 1986, 'Empowering minority students: A framework for intervention', *Harvard Educational Review*, 56(1), pp.18–36 and Jim Cummins, 2000b, *Language, power and pedagogy: Bilingual children in the crossfire*, Clevedon: Multilingual Matters Ltd.

26 Baker, *Foundations of Bilingual Education and Bilingualism*, pp. 406–7.

27 Concha Delgado-Gaitan and Henry Trueba, 1991, *Crossing Cultural Borders*, London and New York: The Falmer Press, p. 138.

28 Baker, *Foundations of Bilingual Education and Bilingualism*, p. 408.

29 Rachel Roberts, 2020, 'A "God-like Science" in Schools' in Christopher J, Hall and Rachel Wicaksono (eds), *Ontologies of English: Conceptualising the language for learning, teaching and assessment*, Cambridge: Cambridge University Press, pp. 122–41, p. 122.

30 Robert Eaglestone, 2002, *Doing English: A Guide for Literature Students*, London and New York, Routledge.

31 Jon Davison and Caroline Daly, 2014, *Learning to Teach English in the Secondary School*, Abingdon: Routledge.

32 Robert Eaglestone, 2002 (2nd edn), *Doing English*, London: Routledge.

33 Roberts, 'A "God-like Science" in Schools', p. 125.

34 Roberts, 'A "God-like Science" in Schools', p. 126.

35 Roberts, 'A "God-like Science" in Schools', p. 126.

36 Roberts, 'A "God-like Science" in Schools', p. 127.

37 Stephen J. Ball, 2017, *The Education Debate*, Bristol: Policy Press, pp. 16–17.

38 Department for Education, 2014, 'English programmes of study: key stage 4 National curriculum in England', *Gov.uk*, https://assets.publishing.service.gov.uk/government/uploads/system/uploads/attachment_data/file/331877/KS4_English_PoS_FINAL_170714.pdf, p. 3, accessed 28.02.2022.

39 Roberts, 'A "God-like Science" in Schools', pp. 130–1.

40 Clare Cunningham, 2020, 'Beliefs about "Good English" in Schools' in Christopher J, Hall and Rachel Wicaksono (eds), *Ontologies of English: Conceptualising the language for learning, teaching*

and assessment, Cambridge: Cambridge University Press, pp. 142–61, p. 144.

41 James Milroy and Lesley Milroy, 1985, *Authority in Language: Investigating Language, Prescription and Standardization*, London: Routledge.

42 Cunningham, 'Beliefs about "Good English" in Schools', p. 144.

43 Neil Murray, 2016, 'An academic literacies argument for decentralizing EAP provision', *ELT Journal*, 70(4), pp. 435–43.

44 T. Herring, 2017, *Standard English in the Primary Classroom: Teachers' Attitudes to Standardised Language*, unpublished undergraduate dissertation, York: York St John University.

45 Peter Garrett, Nikolas Coupland and Angie Williams, 1995, '"City Harsh" and "The Welsh Version of RP": Some ways in which teachers view dialects of Welsh English' in *Language Awareness 1*, 4(2), pp. 99–108.

46 Rebecca S. Wheeler and Rachel Swords, 2004, 'Codeswitching: Tools of language and culture transform the dialectally diverse classroom', *Language Arts*, 81(6), pp. 470–80.

47 Cunningham, 'Beliefs about "Good English" in Schools', p. 149.

48 Eileen H. Tamura, 1996, 'Power, Status, and Hawai'i Creole English: An Example of Linguistic Intolerance in American History', *Pacific Historical Review*, 65(3), pp. 431–54.

49 Karen Grainger, 2013, 'The daily grunt': Middle-class bias and vested interests in the 'Getting in Early' and 'Why Can't They Read?' reports. In *Language and Education*, 27(2), pp. 99–109, p. 107.

50 Cunningham, 'Beliefs about "Good English" in Schools', p. 156.

Period 3: The Arts

Living Beyond Words

> Praise the Lord!
> Praise God in his sanctuary;
>   praise him in his mighty firmament!
> Praise him for his mighty deeds;
>   praise him according to his surpassing greatness!
> Praise him with trumpet sound;
>   praise him with lute and harp!
> Praise him with tambourine and dance;
>   praise him with strings and pipe!
> Praise him with clanging cymbals;
>   praise him with loud clashing cymbals!
> Let everything that breathes praise the Lord!
> Praise the Lord!
> (Psalm 150)

The act of praise that is our lives can be further translated into specific actions of gratitude towards the divine. The recognition, perhaps, that our sense of aloneness emphasized by this world has no reflection in the cosmos. We are not alone. We are held as the stars in the firmament, and we are known. To praise God is to give voice to a deeper understanding that we did not create ourselves or the natural world around us, and that we are part of a chorus of creation which speaks without words. The sanctuary of God is creation itself.

    This speaking without words has already been foregrounded for us in the world we see and from which we draw breath. The splendour and majesty of creation speaks of a God who can do incredible things, bringing wonder and amazement in the big and small acts of love we experience, and in the daily walk towards our fullest selves. There is no sense of limitation with praise. It does not require specific qualifications or training. It is not awarded following a test or exam. Praise of God does not require the permission of others. It is the pulse of creation, which we may ignore and not acknowledge, or of which at times we may not be able to be a part.

Musical instruments only serve to increase our participation in the world around us. Music reveals more language available to us. We enter into a different kind of communication, which may be easier for some and harder for others, but it needs to be made available to all. To speak in music, in noise and sound realigns us with the creative order that does not use words; we are allowed to reconnect beyond what is said and hear what is not said. The different sounds and level of noise underline the truth that we are a part of creation, not set aside from it, not superior to it, but an interdependent part of it.

There is a call to dance, too, to move our bodies beyond the perfunctory and towards a free expression of abandonment in safety and in love. To dance exposes our vulnerability, but it also gives us permission to express ourselves in a communal language that transcends our differences and upholds our common humanity. We dance into and with God because God seeks to dance with us. There is a feeling of rootedness in the divine dance of the Holy Trinity and in the dance of creation speaking back to us. To give the gift of dance is to give the gift of serious and silly fun, the playfulness of God who delights in us, to offer the enjoyment of being alive and to give the opportunity to honour the body and let it speak in a new voice.

For our breath to be able to praise means that it is not suffocated or hindered, and that it is met with the opportunity to be released in joyful affirmation that we are alive, that we have a purpose, and that purpose is love. We can breathe out praise because we were made to breathe in love, not hate, not violence, not exploitation, not abuse. Music and dance offer a different and deep form of human expression. The opportunity to speak without words can be both healing and restorative, can raise us beyond our human inconsistencies to a place of deep mystery and wonder.

* * *

Our art classes at school gave space for some of my classmates to truly shine. We had some brilliant artists in our class and every piece they created drew gasps and admiration from those of us who knew that art was not our key strength or gift. While I felt that my cubist drawing of our kitchen kettle was a great piece for someone of my talent, time has not been kind to this reflection. The reality was I would never take art further than Year 9, but school gave me a love of art that has grown with age.

When I was in my twenties, I saw Picasso's *Guernica* at the Reina Sofia in Madrid, I stood in front of the painting and cried. As a student of Spanish and its history and literature, it felt as if everything I had read about the Spanish Civil War was made human, in black, white and grey tones. I was watching history unfold before my eyes, and was caught in the stare of history's judgement. Every open mouth and troubled stare spoke to me of the reading I had done and the anecdotes professors at St Andrews had told me about this three-year conflict that is still shaping Spain, and its idea of itself, today.

The intense nature of the teenage years, when body and mind are growing and young people are struggling through to find their voice and sense of self, found some room for expression in our drama lessons. Our drama teacher was engaging, and we all enjoyed the lessons in which we were forced to think on our feet and respond to our tasks in pairs and groups. It was a stepping out of the skin, only to be asked to step back into it with a new perspective and deeper learning not only about yourself, but about the world you observed.

My school also offered opportunities to sing in the school choir and learn to play an instrument. I sang badly, but friends and our music teacher were very encouraging. I took up the trombone at first, but moved to the trumpet at the recommendation of our excellent brass teacher. I played the trumpet for a few years, and then stopped. The cost of lessons, the extra hours of practice it was taking, and the need to focus on GCSEs all played a part. At university, finally independent enough to make the decision for myself, I began to play again. And it was joyful, despite my trumpet teacher saying that I had no rhythm, which was a surprise because, 'Black people were supposed to have rhythm'. Regardless of his elderly charm, that comment stayed with me for some time.

The Arts and Humanities

The importance of the arts in education cannot be underestimated and should not be ignored. The problem is that successive governments present a constant and consistent view that arts and humanities subjects do not matter, focusing on narrow outputs and outcomes.

> Official 'targets', 'outcomes' and 'priorities' have very little to do with a genuinely child-centred education. The child at the centre of this 'outcomes' view of education is a cipher or avatar, not a person, while the performative teacher is required to view pedagogy as the science of continuously improving student outcomes and is employed merely to ensure the Ministry can efficiently deliver its core business functions. The interests being served by this sterile vision of learning are governments, not those of children, families and communities.[1]

There has been an arbitrary divide signalling some subjects as academic and others as not, and it is important to interrogate who is saying this and on what evidence are these divisions made. The focus on outcomes and measurable outputs place subjects such as music, drama and art in a straitjacket, condemning them as less valuable and less meaningful. Yet, if we look at our human experience, how many songs do we hold in our minds and hearts that totally transport us to a memory and a place we have treasured? What have been the soundtracks of our lives? How has music led us to new ways of saying and hearing something different or new?

In May 2021, the UK government announced that it would be making a 50 per cent cut to funding of the arts at universities.

> The current plan would affect courses – including music, dance, drama and performing arts; art and design; media studies; and archaeology – that were deemed to not be 'strategic priorities' after a consultation by the Office for Students (OfS) and the education secretary, Gavin Williamson.[2]

This attack on the arts is both dangerous and well-planned. The irrevocable damage this will cause to the education of our children and young people is grave. It reveals deeply myopic thinking and misinforms parents and carers about the value of the arts and humanities.

> It's important to note, especially for parents, that there just isn't a straight line between what you do at school and what you go on to do ... it's like being on the ocean. You keep correcting your course according to things that happen to you. And we end up writing a résumé, which makes it look like it was a plan. There was a study by a professor at Duke University looking at the degree majors for leaders in 500 companies in Silicon Valley.[3] Forty percent were in math, science, or engineering, but 60% were in the arts and humanities.[4]

When there are talks about budget cuts it is always useful to ask what the money is being spent on instead, and what will be the end goal and objective of particular cuts. It is also vital to ask who or what does all this serve? Who wins when our young people cannot study philosophy, history, drama, art, music, theology, or languages? We should be wary of any leadership that seeks to stop questioning and intellectual enquiry about what it means to be human. The reality, for some governments, is that it is far easier to govern a people who are not critically questioning, and interrogating the state of the world and our place in it. The arts offer the space for critical enquiry, for beauty, for transformation, and challenge to the status quo. That is why we need them. It is also important to ask who will be able to continue with these subjects if they are cut from higher education? It will be those who can afford to continue by private means, thereby creating another division in society between the haves and the have-nots.

Music

The study and provision of music in state secondary schools has been on the decline for some time, and many see the English Baccalaureate as a contributing factor:

> The English Baccalaureate or EBacc was brought in by the Coalition Government in 2010 for pupils achieving GCSE grade C or better in English, maths, the sciences, a language and geography or history. The percentages of pupils entering and achieving the EBacc are among several measures used by government to determine a school's performance.
> But critics say this increase has come at the expense of the arts, with just 47.9% of pupils being entered for at least one arts subject in 2016, down from 49.6% the previous year. Researchers, from Sussex University's School of Education and Social Work, surveyed secondary music teachers at 657 state and 48 private schools across England over five years.
> Staff at about 60% of the state schools specifically mentioned the EBacc as causing a negative effect on the provision and uptake of music at their school, while just 3% believed it had benefitted the subject.
> In the five years to 2016–17 the schools in the survey entered fewer students for music qualifications, with schools offering Music BTEC level 2 falling from 166 in 2012–13

to just 50 in 2016–17 and the number offering music GCSE falling by six percentage points – from 85% in 2012–13 to 79% in 2016–17.[5]

The temptation of published league tables and the need to be seen to be improving grades in a school put pressure on both teachers and students to work within the rigidity of the curriculum and government measures for success. Music, therefore, becomes a liability and dispensable, with its value and impact on students' lives dismissed or diminished.

More recently, another report underlined the threat facing music teaching and learning:

> Authors of 'The State of Play' (2019), a report by the Musicians' Union and supported by UK Music and the Music Industries Association, describe music education as being in 'a perilous state'.
> Eight years after ministers published a national plan for music with the aim of ensuring every child had the opportunity to learn a musical instrument, and the establishment of government-funded music hubs – partnerships between schools and arts organisations in their areas – confidence in the government's handling of music education appears to have collapsed in many places ...
> The report paints a picture of creeping cuts to music education, a demoralised workforce with poor employment conditions and huge inequality in instrumental provision, with children from families earning under £28,000 a year half as likely to learn a musical instrument as those with a family income above £48,000. And 89% of parents are making a financial contribution towards instrumental lessons.[6]

There is a sense that there are some subjects that need to be available for all, such as maths, English and science, and then there are other subjects to which only the privileged few should have access. If this is the theory, whether implicit or explicit that is underpinning education policy, again we must ask what is the end goal here? It seems that inequality benefits the ruling class in terms of being able to differentiate between who should rule and who should be ruled. This is not a vision that supports whole-child education or the flourishing of children and young people.

Drama

The 2014 review of the National Curriculum removed drama from the list of statutory subjects:

> The individual programmes of study for key stages 3 and 4 are also available for each subject:
>
> - English (key stages 3 and 4)
> - mathematics (key stages 3 and 4)
> - science (key stage 3 and 4)
> - art and design (key stage 3 only)
> - citizenship (key stages 3 and 4)
> - computing (key stages 3 and 4)
> - design and technology (key stage 3 only)
> - geography (key stage 3 only)
> - history (key stage 3 only)
> - languages (key stage 3 only)
> - music (key stage 3 only)
> - physical education (key stages 3 and 4).[7]

Key stage 3 covers the first three years of secondary education (Years 7, 8 and 9 – ages 11–14) and key stage 4 encompasses the last two years of secondary education (Years 10 and 11 – ages 14–16). Subjects indicated as key stage 3 only are pitted against each other in options at GCSEs. The range of options available at GCSE at any school are entirely dependent on resourcing and whether the school is in favour of the subject and whether the staff and school timetable can accommodate its teaching.

INEQUALITY AND FLOURISHING

Losing drama as part of the National Curriculum, which itself is both limited and restrictive, means that schools facing socio-economic disadvantage may not have funding or space (physical and metaphorical) to offer this subject to their students. It is evident that 'school leaders do not enjoy professional agency with regard to the curriculum, because of the accountability pressures. Very high levels of confidence and capability are required to risk offering curriculum alternatives'.[8] There is also a direct consequence for the diversity of actors the UK presents on the national and global stage:

> Edward Kemp, RADA's director, says the desire for a broader mix of recruits is 'constantly on our radar'. 'It was the reason we originally switched to offering BAs, but then graduate fees came in and we have to charge £9,000 now like everyone else. You plug one hole and another appears.' And he sees changes at secondary schools having an impact.
>
> 'Looking back from 2000 to 2010, the talent pipeline was OK. People were doing drama GCSEs, which is a good guide to the level of interest. Since then there has been a 25% drop in the subject and all of that has fallen away.' Kemp echoes [actor, Irfan] Shamji's concern about reaching schoolchildren before they give up. 'This is what private schools invest in, just in the same way as their playing fields and music provision. That added value is exactly what rich parents look for.'[9]

The reach and depth of talent and potential in children and young people remains untapped. We need to develop an education system that enables learners, regardless of their circumstances, to see themselves afresh, to believe in their own potential and to have the opportunity to see that potential actualised in their most formative years.

In 2012, a copy of Shakespeare's plays read by Nelson Mandela while he was in prison went on display in London.

The book has a cover featuring Hindu deities from Diwali greetings cards, a disguise designed to trick the prison wardens.

The passage Mandela chose as his favourite was from Julius Caesar, just before the Roman statesman leaves for the senate on the Ides of March. It includes the lines: 'Cowards die many times before their deaths/The valiant never taste of death but once.'

Mandela was imprisoned for 27 years during the apartheid years before being released in 1990.[10]

This story is remarkable because it speaks to the power and importance of text and text performed and its relationship with liberation, hope and meaning. The written text of theatre had a place, however small, in the 27 years of imprisonment and helped to sustain a belief in the potential of the human imagination to free us from the injustices and inequalities we have created and to hope for something better. This is not a story about a Black man reading the plays of a dead white man so far removed from his present-day reality, though clearly there is that. Rather, it is about the acknowledgement that the transformative power of the arts is so powerful that even with the threat of punishment, people would take the risk to have access to it. How then are we to judge leaders who try to limit access and turn what is a freedom and a right to an entitlement?

Art

While drama was removed from the National Curriculum, art and design managed to survive the cull.

> In the UK, studying art & design at secondary school is essentially a practice-based endeavour, with external examinations in year 10/11 and year 13. In England, Northern Ireland and Wales, these are the General Certificate of School Education (GCSE) and A-levels respectively; schools in Scot-

land follow a different curriculum and examination system. Following recent reforms to the broader curriculum, intended, to use the words of then-Education Secretary Michael Gove (2012), to 'restore rigour' and instil 'the skills and knowledge needed for the modern workplace and advanced study', a written component was mandated in these two assessments. At GCSE level, this takes the form of a requirement for students to include 'written annotations' in their sketchbooks or portfolios. At A-level, it involves written annotations and a 'continuous narrative' of 1,000–3,000 words submitted as part of an in-depth practical body of work. Beyond this, individual schools may set their own assessments. Both GCSE and A-level examinations and their supporting courses of study are controlled by a series of independent exam boards, principal among them AQA, Edexcel, OCR and WJEC.[11]

While the existence of art and design may seem like a win, barriers have been placed within the subject that hinder teachers and students. The introduction of the written component disadvantaged students for whom the articulation of their artistic thought and production in words was a struggle. Further there have been challenges in understanding what was required and how to best prepare children and young people for this additional assessment:

> It is a confusing picture, with information and clear examples difficult to find in the various exam board documents, and, from the accounts of the teachers interviewed, in the training provided by the exam boards for teachers, examiners and moderators. Mixed in with this lack of clarity and consistency about what is required were concerns about why. Rather than serving as a tool for students, writing, the teachers felt, was more often being used as a proof for others – not just as proof of the students' thinking and process, but also as a proof of art as a 'serious' subject in the curriculum and/or as conforming with standardised regimes of assessment and practice.[12]

PERIOD 3: THE ARTS

The need for frameworks against which some learning can be measured and reviewed does not mean that subjects should be sacrificed at the altar of assessment and misconceptions about their value. What happened to enjoyment and fun and play with learning and through which learning can be embedded as a lifelong objective and skill? Who says art is not a 'serious' subject, or is not 'serious' in the state sector and only considered valuable in independent schools? If art helps us to decipher process and understand the world around us, does it, therefore, not have value for our growth as individuals and as a society. The ability to review and reflect and engage with a creative piece engenders critical thinking. Or is it that our government prefers automata who cannot engage with the questioning that is needed to unearth injustice and hold our leaders accountable?

Creativity

In 2019, 'The Durham Commission was convened to look at how our education system and wider system of learning for children can grow that capacity for creativity.'[13] Yet another report and yet more recommendations, the implementation of which may now be sidelined as a result of the undeniable impact of Covid-19 on education in the UK. The report did not say anything new, but used research well to present its case for creativity in teaching and learning in schools:

> The report, put together in collaboration with academics from Durham University, concludes that creativity is not something that should inhabit the school curriculum only as it relates to drama, music, art and other obviously creative subjects, but that creative thinking ought to run through all of school life, infusing the way human and natural sciences are learned.[14]

It was important that the report highlighted that the notion of creativity was not limited to the arts. Rather 'creativity exists in all disciplines. It is valued by mathematicians, scientists and entrepreneurs, as well as by artists, writers and composers.'[15] The report also recognized the challenge of making creativity central within the current education system that is both restrictive and reductive:

> The National Curriculum in England (Department for Education, 2014) does not currently require schools to focus on teaching for creativity although one of its two aims mention the concept ... This draws attention to the creative achievements of singular individuals in the past and the outcomes or products of creativity in terms of these big achievements but does not focus on encouraging the creative processing of learners.[16]

The idea that creativity can encourage and lead to interdisciplinary work and thinking was already highlighted by the Church of England, as the report indicates: 'There can, of course, be inter-relationships between subjects, as recognised by the Church of England's Vision for Education (2016) which explicitly identifies creativity as being part of all subjects in its 4,700 schools.'[17]

Yet the challenge remains that children and young people are funnelled through an education system that is focused on specialization. Choosing specific subjects at aged 16 and then again at aged 18 for study at university is the ultimate goal. There is little room for interdisciplinarity and plurality of thought if you simply want a human being that is productive in one area or two at the very most. To be a polymath is not celebrated and to be able to develop a curiosity that leads to an exploration of ideas is frowned upon if it takes away from the study towards assessments. The system does not welcome or promote creativity because its focus is on measurable outputs not on flourishing and encouraging children and young people to be their fullest selves:

PERIOD 3: THE ARTS

In England, there is a very structured programme of formal testing and examinations. Pupils in Key Stage 1 take Standardised Assessment Tests (SATs) in mathematics and English during year 2. In Key Stage 2 they take SATs tests in English, maths and science in year 6. At age 15 or 16, young people in secondary schools take General Certificate of Secondary Education (GCSE) exams, and Advanced Level (A level) or Business and Technology Education Council (BTEC) examinations occur normally at 18 or 19 years of age. In addition, a number of alternative post-16 vocational opportunities and qualifications are also available, including apprenticeships.[18]

The current system in which children and young people are the most tested students in history must end. This is neither good for the mental health and well-being of the children and young people nor does it offer them the best deal in terms of what they get from their school experience. Instead of being invested in, with gifts, abilities and capacities nurtured, the result is labelling and ignoring or displacing the potential of many young people who do not test well or whose potential is diminished by this rigidity and lack of vision. What we have, therefore, is a need for creativity to be placed at the heart of our education system in order to liberate the mind and the potential of children and young people as well as create and develop notions of interdisciplinary teaching and learning that equip and excite learners to respond imaginatively to some of the challenges we face at local, national and international levels.

Reimagining the arts

Arts and humanities are not the poor relation of science, technology, engineering and maths (STEM). The presentation of subjects on opposing ends of an artificial spectrum is both erroneous and deeply troubling because a hierarchy of knowledge is created, with importance linked to funding and investment as we have seen over decades. Further it roots children in misinformation and encourages binary divisions within learning that do a disservice to the notion of education and to what it can achieve for individuals and communities.

Let us reimagine an education system infused with creativity and the message that to be creative is not limited to a particular subject. There is a celebration of the arts and humanities and their interconnectedness with other subjects and areas of learning. If music, drama and art are welcomed, invested in and nurtured among learners in school, then this would facilitate a deeper understanding of creative expression, and its ability to transform and enable new ways of seeing and interpreting the world.

The major global challenges we face as a human race, not least the current international health crisis which may last this entire decade, cannot be solved within one subject area or with siloed thinking. We will miss key innovations and the opportunity to alleviate human suffering more quickly and in a more sophisticated way. Studying the arts should be freely available to every child and young person until the age of 18, with a clear indication of how the creative arts intersect with other subjects. Children and young people could have an 'arts passport' that encouraged engaging in and production of the arts, developing their knowledge and exposure to the creative industries. The idea of learning as a journey would be reinforced through criteria for engagement that matched local provision and encouraged local arts organizations to work more systematically with schools to develop their learning and understanding of the subjects' impact beyond school. Arts Collectives, a new funded initiative by the government, could engage children and young people to respond to local challenges through art in order to find creative solutions for expressing their lived experience, their agency and their ability to create the kind of communities they want to see and in which they want to live.

PERIOD 3: THE ARTS

Notes

1 Stephen J. Ball, 2017, *The Education Debate*, Bristol: Policy Press, pp. 58–9.
2 Lanre Bakare, 2021, '"Strategic misstep": arts education cuts risk UK cultural leadership, government told', *The Guardian*, 12 May, www.theguardian.com/education/2021/may/12/tragic-misstep-arts-education-cuts-risk-uk-cultural-leadership-government-told, accessed 28.02.2022.
3 Vivek Wadhwa, Richard B. Freeman and Ben A. Rissing, 2008, 'Education and Tech Entrepreneurship, (1 May), available at SSRN: https://ssrn.com/abstract=1127248, accessed 28.02.2022.
4 Anne Sweeney in conversation with Sir Ken Robinson, 2013, 'Every Child is an Artist', *Fast Company*, 8 May, www.fastcompany.com/3014819/disney-anne-sweeney-sir-ken-robinson, accessed 28.02.2022.
5 Judith Burns, 2017, 'Music "could face extinction" in secondary schools', *BBC News*, 9 March, www.bbc.co.uk/news/education-39154242, accessed 28.02.2022.
6 Fiona Millar, 2019, 'School music report reveals cuts, inequality and demoralised teachers', *The Guardian*, 2 April, www.theguardian.com/education/2019/apr/02/school-music-cuts-inequality-demoralised-teachers, accessed 28.02.2022.
7 UK Government, 'National curriculum in England: secondary curriculum', *Gov.uk*, www.gov.uk/government/publications/national-curriculum-in-england-secondary-curriculum, accessed 28.02.2022.
8 Gemma Parker and David Leat, 2021, 'The Case of Curriculum Development in England: Oases in a Curriculum Desert' in Mark Priestley, Daniel Alvunger, Stavroula Philippou and Tiina Soini (eds), *Curriculum Making in Europe: Policy and Practice Within and Across Diverse Contexts*, Bingley: Emerald Publishing, pp. 151–74, p. 159.
9 Vanessa Thorpe, 2018, 'Why does British theatre leave working-class actors in the wings?', *The Guardian*, 8 July.
10 BBC, 2012, 'Nelson Mandela's Shakespeare edition to go on display', *BBC News*, 19 June, www.bbc.co.uk/news/entertainment-arts-18502371, accessed 28.02.2022.
11 Jennifer Blunden, 2019, 'Bridge or Barrier? Writing in Secondary Art & Design Education in the UK', *The International Journal of Art & Design*, 38(4), pp. 916–26, p. 917.
12 Blunden, 'Bridge or Barrier?', p. 919.
13 University of Durham, 2019, *Durham Commission on Creativity and Education*, www.dur.ac.uk/resources/creativitycommission/DurhamReport.pdf, p. 5, accessed 28.02.2022.

14 Editorial, 2019, 'The Guardian view on creativity in schools: a missing ingredient', *The Guardian*, 18 October.
15 University of Durham, *Durham Commission on Creativity and Education*, p. 6.
16 University of Durham, *Durham Commission on Creativity and Education*, p. 53.
17 University of Durham, *Durham Commission on Creativity and Education*, p. 53.
18 University of Durham, *Durham Commission on Creativity and Education*, p. 54.

INTERVIEW WITH REVD CANON DR JOANNA COLLICUTT, PRIEST, CHARTERED CLINICAL PSYCHOLOGIST AND REGISTERED SPECIALIST NEUROPSYCHOLOGIST, UNIVERSITY LECTURER

9 October 2020

JC: I do have a lot of sympathy with the idea that we are not educating people, we are programming them.

I was thinking about it the other day. In four years, I went to four different schools because of my parents moving me around, my mother having a *very* fixed notion – I don't know if you know this, but my mother was an immigrant to this country. She was Indian. She married my father when he was fighting in the Burma campaign in the Second World War. She came back and she had two ways on which she was on the outside: one was racially but actually that was for her, although important, she was more passionate about the gender side. She had two daughters and she was really passionate that we would get the best education.

Her idea was that, as a woman, you have to get yourself in a position where you can call the shots, and [where you] are not dependent on other people. You have to have what she would recognize as a profession so that you couldn't simply be laid off ... but that you had a unique contribution to make.

And so, because of that, when we lived in Manchester, she kind of moved me out of what was a really good state school and used all her savings to send me to a private school, and then we moved house. I had to go to two different kinds of private schools around the age of 11, which were very small-minded and not particularly expansive. And then was lucky enough to go to an all-girls school, where all the staff were women, most of them single. If they got married, they were out really. They were kind of tolerated but that was looked at as not fully being committed to your vocation. And we had some men come in to do certain things. Interestingly, we had priests come in to teach religious studies (RS). And we had a male physics teacher, I think, because 'we are girls'. And the ethos of that school was very much, you can be what you want to be. Gender isn't an issue because 'we're all girls'. And then I went on to an all-women's college at Oxford because, well, it was so long ago, but [at the time] women weren't allowed to join men's colleges. So there's something there about a particularly protected environment and the ethos was an ethos, and I reflect on it a lot, of whole-person education. [The school] had very high academic standards, but they could have been higher if they had neglected some of the whole-person stuff that they were doing. Their overall aim was to build, I suppose we might call it character, but to build women who were fully themselves. It had a very high kind of ethos of public service: 'You took an exam to get into this school, you're gifted and the reason you're gifted is because you have to put back into society. This is not your gift.'

It was a kind of low-level, it was informed by some kind of liberal, I guess, low-level Christian ethos. In a sense, your gifts and knowledge are not your own, that you are kind of stewards of these things. The school motto was 'honour wisdom'. And, of course, wisdom is a female figure anyway. The important thing was to build wisdom, and to build wise people who would be good citizens, who would be great scholars, but whose scholarship was not the important thing. The important thing was to be who you were meant to be. And a lot of that was marked by service and self-sacrifice. There were some good things about that, loads of good things about that, and increasingly I am appreciating it, but there are some darker sides to it, as there always are. But what I often reflect on is how you rarely see that ethos now, it seems to me.

And when I went to university, it was *there*, in certain pockets within the university. There was also a real sense when I went to university of learning for its own sake. And that was always the mantra at school as well: 'You don't learn instrumentally. You don't learn in order to pass an exam. You don't learn in order to be a better person. You don't learn in order to build up your self-esteem. You learn for the joy of it.' And it was always a sense of trying to instil joy in scholarship. And when I came to Oxford back in the seventies, that was there too. I don't find that now. It seems totally instrumental to me. You learn in order to pass a degree, in order to fit you better for life, in some way shape or form, which is to do largely with employment, I think. But, also, with kind of building a sense of self-worth.

Psychologists talk about extrinsic and intrinsic reward and extrinsic and intrinsic motivation. To instil a habit of intrinsic motivation is probably what my school was doing. And I think that is kind of gone. And with intrinsic motivation, which you see in 'flow states',[1] they're intrinsically motivated. Gordon Allport, years ago in the forties and fifties, looked at religion and asked the question: is there a difference between religion that's intrinsically motivated and religion that is extrinsically motivated? So, you go to church for social networking purposes, because it is a respectable thing to do in your community, or in order to get something out of it that is inherently rewarding. So that extrinsic and intrinsic stuff has been around a lot in areas of happiness research. And one of the things about extrinsic motivation is that you need to keep getting rewards to keep yourself motivated. Whereas intrinsic motivation is self-generating. And so, if you're a very extrinsic person or if you're in a very extrinsic culture, you're more at risk of depression. Because if those rewards stop coming you have nothing interior to give you joy.

I don't know whether, if you did a really systematic study,

you would see hard data to support this, but my impression is that that intrinsic aspect of learning has gone. Definitely in my undergrad teaching at Oxford but also in the ethos of the way we are expected to teach. You see it in the culture of the students, but I think that they pick that up from the institutions themselves. And I have seen a shift in the way schools are. I don't think there are many schools that would be like the schools I went to.

I just live with the fact that we have to have learning outcomes, for example, in our teaching at [theological college]. Or the type of feedback forms that the students are required to fill in. There's a whole area of practical theology ... where the only value in what you're doing, and we see this in our feedback forms, is: 'How is this going to work out in my ministry? How will I use this instrumentally?' Two things about that: you don't know how you're going to use it. My experience is that I've had students ten years later who say, 'I was really bored in your session on this, but actually something came up in my parish and I thought: that was useful. I went back to the notes and it's really, really helped me'. So, you don't know immediately ... But secondly, I don't think that is what education is about. Maybe it is, but that is not where I am coming from.

MIB: What's your definition of education?

JC: What I want to do is, I want to inspire people primarily to get some kind of joy in whatever the subject is. It's easier to inspire people with joy in teaching about the gospel because it's fundamental. You're meant to have joy in the gospel! But if I were just teaching academic psychology, or whatever subject it is, I would want to inspire them to take joy in it. To be curious, to think: 'I could step into this and I won't drown, and I could find a way through that would enhance my life, and that I would carry through into old age, when all these exterior things about the usefulness of the study cease to be pressures on me because I am not trying to find a job any more'.

What I want to do, I think, is to get people interested in the subject. I don't do this on purpose, but I do use a lot of humour in my teaching. I think what humour does – real laughter – it lifts your arousal levels.[2] It opens your mind to look at things from more than one perspective. It allows you to make connections with the ordinary. I suppose that's the other thing. Somebody once said to me, you bring the domestic into the classroom quite a lot. I didn't notice that I did but when I thought about it, I do. I think that's to do with the fact that the learning you do in the classroom is meant to be connected to the whole of life. And I don't think that's the same as saying that it has to be applied to a practical problem. It comes out of life and it feeds back into life. I think that indicates that the principles you're talking about have more traction than just in the classroom. It's a network of wisdom. So I will discipline myself to have some learning outcomes, but I do hate that whole thing.

MIB: Yes, it is standard practice.

JC: I would rather just say: by the end of this session you will be inspired to maybe read a bit more, to be curious about an idea that came up in the session, and make connections with some of the other stuff that you are working on. I can remember once talking about something in a seminar and somebody said, 'Oh, I think Becky said something about that the other week.' And I was just delighted! And we kind of stopped and I said, 'That's exactly what we could be looking for, not these silos of learning' … which relates to your point [in our pre-interview conversation] about interdisciplinarity and specialization, which I think is really interesting.

So, I want to inspire and I want to stretch, which is why I always teach probably about a level higher from the module level, as given. And you know, what we say at theological college is, it's OK to teach at a higher level as long as you don't mark at a higher level than the module. Because I think that people need to be given a vision. I think it's that, giving a vision of what this could mean to them. And giving tools to know where to go for the knowledge, and to be given permission to think critically and analytically, confidently about data and [the] challenge that they will discover. Because situations will change, but the principles won't change. You can still bring those to bear.

I read this book called *A Mathematician's Apology*, which was written in the 1940s by G. H. Hardy. And it's a bit idiosyncratic but it's basically a kind of defence of pure mathematics. And it's kind of saying: 'the point of pure mathematics is not what can it do for me, in the way that applied mathematics ... The point of applied mathematics is that it tells you stuff about the real world. Whereas pure mathematics is a bit more of a mental game.' And one of the points he made, which I thought was really interesting, was that pure mathematics often has real world implications. But that does not validate it. So, you don't judge it by the fact that it is useful. It often is useful, but in its own right. It has validity whether or not it turned out to be useful.

The argument is around the nature of truth and the importance of beauty, and I was so struck by it, really, because I like pure mathematics and I never used to like applied maths. I actually thought you might be able to take that argument and start to play with it in relation to theology as well. Is there an excuse for the rough equivalent of pure theology as opposed to practical theology? What would it look like? What would your criteria be? I actually think that platonic triangle of justice, beauty and truth as reflecting the good is a really good lens to look at things. And it has often been used to look at education. If you leave out beauty, I think you're in trouble. And it's obvious in a way that the things you've talked about ... drama, music, the creative arts – that would be the other thing I'd really want to *try* to instil in people is some degree of creativity – it's obvious in a way that these things engage with beauty. But, actually, so do science and mathematics. And beauty has to be, I think it's part of wisdom, and it's part of wisdom because wisdom is embodied and it is about craft, certainly in the Hebrew Bible, but I think everybody agrees that it is something about crafting life well. And integration of the home and the workplace and the body and the mind, and the practical and the theoretical.

MIB: I am struck by the overlaps with the current discussion about taking poetry out of the curriculum and removing some of the arts because they have no validity: 'retraining professionals because obviously their jobs are not viable because [again] they have no validity ...' I think it's very easy to slide into dangerous territory when we start to say, actually, some things don't have value unless there is a practical, applied output.

JC: Absolutely. And it's a bit like the 'I thought your sessions were boring and then ten years later, I found that they were useful.' We just don't know, and we have to live with not being able to measure that and have that degree of prior intuition that these things are useful, valuable, if not useful. And one of the things that strikes me is that (I like all the arts, but I am probably most involved in music) a lot of musicians, a lot of very, very strong amateur musicians, are also medics or scientists. There are lots of stories of medics who gave up medicine. There was one I was looking at in the summer [of 2020] of somebody who came back into medicine because of the Covid-19 situation, who had left it to be a professional musician.

So, these are not two areas that are far apart ... We're talking about whole individuals but we're also this body of Christ thing – the whole of society. Everybody has a place. You could just take it straight out of 1 Corinthians. No part of the body is less valuable than another part of the body. They all need each other. And I think that relates to this thing about specialization that you talked about as well. I wrote a chapter [recently in which] I just talk about this impression that I had from talking to young people, that it's very, very stressful when they get to the point around – it's quite hard choosing GCSE courses and it gets very hard when you have to choose what you're going to do in the sixth form. The very thing you said about cutting off parts of yourself, and it relates to your identity, and you have to at a very early age, prematurely, say 'I am this kind of animal'. So, it's a bit autobiographical in a way, though I don't say that. But when I was at school, I was really good at everything, I have to say, apart from games, at which I was absolutely crap. It was quite difficult for me to choose, even at GCSE, it was quite difficult to choose things, but I knew what I wanted to do. I wanted to do classics, which I probably wouldn't have been good at. I wanted to study ancient Greek and do something around classics or ancient history at university. And my parents just wouldn't let me. They said, 'If you can do science, you need to do science because who's going to give you a job with your poncy classics degree.' So it was straight back to: 'You have got to be employable. You've got to do the three sciences and you will not do Greek!'

What happens is that at the age of 45, I take a career break out of my largely science-driven profession and do the Oxford Postgraduate Diploma in Theology and I do New Testament Greek there, and now I use it all the time. When I worked at Heythrop [College] you saw this all the time with these mature students. Their story was: I wanted to do this from when I was a child and they wouldn't let me and now I've got the money or the time, and I'm bloody well going to do it. Equally, they [my school] didn't let me do art because they said only the dim girls did it. So you can see that there were dark sides to this school! And as you know, two or three years ago, I did an MA in Christianity and the Arts because it was a great passion of mine ... It's a symptom of how young people are squeezed. And it wasn't bad for me and it wasn't very traumatic. But it's clearly impacted on my life. And there's an entry in one of my diaries that I've kept from when I was about 14. I said, 'Went to the careers fair today. Mum dragged me from place to place. Doesn't she understand I want to be a vicar!' And I was in the end. But many people don't have the chances and advantages that I have had ... It is a part of people's story, this kind of grief of who I might have been.

INTERVIEW

MIB: I think there is something also about the fact that the trauma is sometimes unprocessed for people who don't have the ability to go back to what it is they always wanted to do. And I remember speaking to a lady ... when I was living in Kent, [and she was] saying how traumatic it was that she failed her 11-plus. And it's stayed with her ever since. Because she couldn't go to the grammar school and, therefore, she feels that there's this other life that would have been had she not failed the 11-plus. But it was a judgement on her person, not on her intellect.

JC: I see that a lot with elderly parishioners. I mean two things: one is you have to be careful how you do teaching with them. Because if you make it too much like a school situation, the ones who failed the 11-plus actually start to get almost flashbacks. And a whole lot of stuff comes back about 'I am not good enough. I could have been this' ... You know, for some of us school has been a great experience ... There are lot of people of that generation for whom it's been a place where you were told that you weren't worth it ... There are some horrendous stories.

MIB: There are. And I think I struggle a lot with this having been a Head of Careers and working with young people, one-to-one, having young people cry in my office about being forced to do a subject that they didn't want to do. I had a young man [in my office] once. I was told that he wanted to do art and drama ... He's clearly brilliant [at these subjects]. You could tell that this was what he loved. And he said to me, 'Well, you know, my parents have already laid down the tracks and I am just on the train.' I never forgot that. I was so moved. I think I came home and cried because I couldn't believe that sense of loss of freedom so young. You know, and we have this romantic view that young people: 'They bounce back; they're young; they won't remember it; it's all fine; in ten years' time they won't even remember the fact that they were 16'. That's not my experience of young people.

INEQUALITY AND FLOURISHING

JC: If you look over people's memories over a lifetime there are certain areas that they remember very, very strongly ... if you look at older people, with whom I have done quite a lot of work, the stories that will come up will be stories from those times, all around identity and worth.

MIB: I think Covid has thrown up for me quite a lot of questions that I've had in my head, you know, [for example] a whole generation were not tested for a whole year and mercifully somehow they have got through it. But we've set these absolutes that don't seem to be necessarily in the best interest of the young person. [Rather] it's about us measuring ourselves as adults and as capable institutions.

JC: Yes, and mental health – such a minefield. I think I'd go back to what I said about education being in part, you know, in the coalface of the classroom, about instilling joy and intrinsic delight, and cultivating that in people. And I do think that creativity and the way you use [time] ... break time, the lunch time, and the non-academic, *allegedly*, subject times. They're all about building a kind of fitness – I don't really want to call it resilience – that makes you less likely to become unwell mentally ... I am not a great fan of thinking about distress in terms of sickness. I think it only gets you so far. And it does also lead you to look for medical solutions whereas in fact the solutions are likely to be multiple and very much based around culture.

So just as you need a healthy kind of diet to stop you getting physically unwell, you need a healthy kind of ethos, which would include, I think, cultivation of joy, something about intrinsic self-worth. So, getting away from these ideas of 'our worth is based on how you did in your exams, or how you look'. It's very easy to say that [but] implementing it, of course, is a difficult one, especially in the context of social media. That ramps everything up in a way that it never did even ten years ago. I think, rather than pathologizing the kind of distress that we see – you will see people who have full-blown diagnosable psychiatric conditions – but I think there's a lot of stuff that's subclinical around, and a lot of stuff that is subclinical that is made clinical because that's just an easy way of labelling it, whereas in fact the distress is more existential and it reflects the culture.

One thing is around intrinsic, inherent joy, and another is about intrinsic self-worth and self-worth that is not predicated on other things, that are external. And the other thing is working intentionally on questions of identity without politicizing them. Perhaps they have been politicized because they weren't given enough mainstream attention earlier ... I think [having] some actual didactic-values-education. This is just me just being old fashioned. I don't think a system where you say everything goes works, or every perspective on a problem is equally valid. There are some things where you say that isn't acceptable. And it starts really early on in parenting. If one of my children picks up a brick and slams it down on the other one, that is just not acceptable. There is no way from any perspective that that is OK. Some things in society that are not OK, so hate, what we're now recognizing as hate, but you would have to unpack that more.

There is the not-OK version of that, but the other side of that coin is: what are the fundamental non-negotiables? One is the equal value of all people. And I am not sure that that is presented systematically enough in the positive sense rather than in the 'we shouldn't hate' sense and instilled there in the curriculum ... Something about non-negotiable moral values that a community has come to some kind of consensus on, that are spelled out right from the beginning. Because unless you develop that habitus that there are some things that are just not OK, and you're left kind of floating, then you have no critical lens. It is not [just] that you want to train people to not go down certain roads. It's like heresy really. You don't tell people 'Don't think this', but you say, 'If you think this, the consequences of it will be this. You need to be incredibly careful. It's a very dangerous road to go down.' And I think people are anxious about imposing a moral framework from the top because we are in a pluralistic society, but I think it can be done. I think a consensus can be reached about what is good, that doesn't have to be driven by religion or a particular moral stance. There are some basic non-negotiables.

Those things, I think, in the longer sense play into mental health issues because ... most mental health issues boil down to certain key questions around: 'Am I worth anything? What's the right thing to do? Who am I? Is there a purpose or a point, is there any meaning in life?' That's the other thing, *meaning* – so it's existential. And the only way they differ is the degree to which you employ defences against really upsetting answers to those questions. Or you actually have reached really upsetting answers to those questions. For example, 'I am worthless', and the way you balance those, and the kind of form of working those through that they take. In a way the surface symptoms, although they seem variable, the core issues at the bottom of them are always the same ... And I think everyone needs meaning. I think people are agreed on that now. And the way we make meaning is very often through the creative arts. And that is part of their value.

MIB: Yes, absolutely.

JC: I suppose the other point, to relate to your stuff about the school year, is also about the school day. One other big way we make meaning is by making community, and the schools become almost proxy families for so many children. And the fact that the school day is extended with after school clubs and breakfast clubs and things. The family is the place where you eat. And perhaps, for some children, school is the only place where you sit round a table. So [we need] a rediscovery of the value of hospitality as a value in school, of school as hospital not in the sense of curing sick people, but in offering hospitality. When you look at lunchtime, it's not just about the physical food. It's about the way it's consumed and where you do it, and how that links into other values about community.

INTERVIEW

And then that links into your question about the school holiday and the nature of the terms.

MIB: That is a really interesting lens.

JC: And I connect with what you say about the six weeks in the summer, which in our rural setting where I am (I actually did a reflection in the summer saying, 'Well, I think it's a good thing'!), but I absolutely accept that it doesn't even mirror ... the rural community. It's a historic thing, but it [also] doesn't mirror an urban community. And it does have this element of frontloading people ... so that they [educators] are absolutely exhausted by Christmas time if not before ... and then having this period in the summer where, during the lockdown, kids were not getting enough food, a lot of them. Yes, I think it needs rebalancing.

MIB: ... I think there's also something again about codifying education within specific timeframes. Whereas actually we haven't quite grasped the notion of lifelong learning. Arguably, I think that some countries have done a bit better, in saying actually: 'You're learning all the time. And if we say that there's perhaps formal learning happening during periods, why does it only have to be 39 weeks? And for students for whom home is not safe, there is a very difficult place that they are going mentally every holiday, when school is their refuge, when school is where they go to be safe from what is happening at home. And then suddenly we're saying, 'Well you have to be at home'. Why? *Why?* I think we've got this all wrong, I really do ... I feel that it's gone away from being the child at the centre to some sort of [educational] institutional juggernaut whereby decisions can be made by algorithms and nobody is thinking about the child [as was the case with the exam results fiasco in 2020]. Nobody is thinking that we've told them that they are not worthy based on exams result that were created by a computer, based on historical data, within the context of the young person *not* having taken an exam. We've told them they've failed an exam they never took!

JC: It's awful. That generation have now gone into university ... And that whole thing about the university experience, and that's the other thing that's really shifted is that the student is the purchaser of a commodity now. [They think] from a consumer, commercial point of view, 'what have you given me at the end of your lecture that I can say made it worth putting my money into it', which of course is the ultimate extrinsic motivator for doing anything ... so they go up [to university] expecting to have this experience. I have no idea what this experience is meant to be, but because it's been turned into a commodity, they then feel that they've been done by very badly by paying out their money and not having whatever this experience was. Whereas in fact the process is not about that.

They [students] have been treated terribly, abusively really [during this pandemic], but losing the experience is the least problematic part of it. It is a really weird narrative to have. There are all sorts of things that perhaps if you unpacked that seem to be important, like making new social contacts, learning to live independently away from home. I think one of the things they're not getting, which I think is so interesting is face-to-face teaching. They don't know what it is they're missing but I think I know what it is they're missing. And it's about embodied wisdom again. It's about: 'I was in a room with this person who embodies and holds something that I want to be.' And we know that from research on [the subject of] wisdom, is that people don't get it from books. And I don't think they're going to get it from online seminars. They get it from other people.

MIB: But [as an educator] you're authentic and I think there's a challenge with the digital. I have no social media, which is a very intentional decision, because it's performative, and I think that there is a real challenge to somebody that wants to engage with an authentic human being. Whether or not they agree with them, they will still recognize that that person is being authentic, authentically themselves. And I think that children do that brilliantly. They just know. Certainly, I mean I can't be in a classroom of 25 teenagers and sort of perform my way through it. They will know. Because that is why they connect with the subject, with your authenticity in delivering a subject that you also love.

JC: Yes, that's completely it. If you let yourself be authentic, it's much less hard work than being performative. I think about these kids that have gone up to university now, locked into their halls of residence in a way that is absolutely disgraceful.

MIB: I think there is something about universities having to interrogate how to come out of this with a sense of integrity about what their historic mission was. Because I think, if we go back and we end it with where we started, about the purpose of education, I think that young people are going to be questioning, 'Well, do I need university at all? Do I need institution? If this is what they've done to me, if this is how I have been treated.' And they will start the comparison with young people who are doing apprenticeships, young people who have taken other routes and they will say, 'Well this didn't happen to them!'

JC: A key thing, one last thing, in the old universities, Oxford and Cambridge and some others, that was the origin of the word fellowship. And I think if you go back to what that word 'fellowship' means, it was about being in a company of learners, embodied learners in a community. We now use fellowship in a purely, you know, 'I've got my fellowship.' It's a job. It's an academic marker. It's a real clue to us about what education should be like …

MIB: … I start this book with the idea that we are in front of the empty tomb and I think there's a huge part of this year [2020] and certainly with education … that you've been allowed to forget because of the weightiness of this year, that we are in front of the empty tomb, with all that energy and potential and light, as you say, and permission. This is what I hope we can take into the next five to ten years of questioning about what should our secondary education system look like. Because it's the empty tomb. It's not just the cross. And that is a huge responsibility. It is a *huge* responsibility, and I don't think we see it as a responsibility. We see education as political pawn. But in that empty tomb is the potentiality of every young person, and I cannot understand how we've got to a place where we say some young people are more valuable than others. And that whole notion permeates every institution we create relating to young people.

JC: It is a sin actually, to use a Christian term. It's the human condition ... Unless we intentionally fight it, we revert to that.

Notes

1 Headspace, 'Popularized by positive psychologists Mihaly Csikszentmihalyi and Jeanne Nakamura, flow state describes a feeling where, under the right conditions, you become fully immersed in whatever you are doing.' See www.headspace.com/articles/flow-state.

2 In psychology, this means the state of being alert, awake and attentive.

Period 4: Sports

Starting the Race Fairly

> Therefore, since we are surrounded by so great a cloud of witnesses, let us also lay aside every weight and the sin that clings so closely, and let us run with perseverance the race that is set before us, looking to Jesus the pioneer and perfecter of our faith, who for the sake of the joy that was set before him endured the cross, disregarding its shame, and has taken his seat at the right hand of the throne of God.
> (Hebrews 12.1–2)

To be able to thrive, we need support. We need the daily affirmation of love that testifies to a belief in, and an upholding of, us as we embark on the journeys of our lives. There needs to be the emotional, psychological and physical scaffolding that provides nourishment, protection and guidance. To be supported is to be looked out for, and to have others anticipate some of the road ahead, not for self-interest but for the sole purpose of enabling the flourishing and well-being of others.

It is clear that not all people in our world have this support, and this lack of equality means that the start of any journey is already weighed down by unequal provision that stifles potential and limits opportunities. Sometimes the shame and wrongs we carry are not our own, but those imposed on us, those that have been done to us, by others, by society, by our communities. All the weight, and shame and wrongs clasp us within a broken view of ourselves and of our purpose, of what we can be and who we are a called to be, having been made in God's image.

The journeys of life in which there are struggles for self-actualization are not the same for all. Some journeys are longer, and some are much harder. The journey set for some can be more favourable to flourishing, while the journey set for others can wilfully hinder flourishing. All journeys are contextualized by human structures and systems. Recognizing this means we can work to amend and adjust our world to give an equitable start for all. The expectations of endurance are misplaced if they do not take into account the start of the journey, or the conditions around which individuals have had to take their first steps.

The compass of Jesus Christ refocuses our endeavours on a greater calling and purpose: to walk and run and skip towards our inheritance as children of God. The full flourishing of our lives is shaped by the path we have to walk and travel, and the conditions of the journey we experience. As we embark on being fully alive and fully ourselves in love, we remember that this love was first expressed towards us by God and made manifest in the life, death and resurrection of Jesus Christ. No journey is beyond God's understanding and presence. No path is so solitary and shame-filled that it cannot have Jesus as a companion. If we look to the cross and then the empty tomb, we are held in the responsibility to reassess the start lines in the journeys of life, set back so far for so many from where they should be, and to see the gift of transformation we have been given by the Holy Spirit. The race that has been set by human structures and systems can be unset, redrawn, reimagined for the flourishing of all.

***

It was all about netball at school, which may be something of a surprise when you know my true height is four feet eleven inches and three quarters. I have neither the stature of a champion or the shooting skills of medal winners, but I did have agility and a spring that lifted me high into the air, and the ability to lead a team. I was captain of the netball team and it was so much fun to play and win and, yes, sometimes lose. I was Centre, or Wing Attack for most matches and sometimes moving to Wing Defence, if and when needed. The key was to support my team whenever needed. I was rarely the star, but so many lessons can be learned just by being on the court. To be present and to have the resource of a court and a hall in which to play meant that we could learn; learn about ourselves as individuals and about what made us a good team.

The reality is my secondary school had several playgrounds and an indoor hall that could be used for sport. It was timetabled in and there were opportunities to play after school also. As girls our bodies mattered, and they mattered to us. They were under our microscopic gaze as growing teenagers. We had no social media then so there was perhaps less focus on the aesthetic. Though it mattered that we were fit and healthy and that we could 'keep up' in PE. The physical education (PE) teachers were a mixed bunch. We were a boisterous and athletic class and deeply competitive. So sometimes things went to the wire needing teacher intervention, and sometimes we just needed to let off hormonal steam. I took for granted that every child had access to the space we had and the teachers who were qualified PE teachers, not other teachers roped in to do PE. We were offered sports that we could play within the confines of our school grounds.

PE in secondary schools

PE is a part of the National Curriculum. This means that time is allocated for sport and physical well-being from ages 11–16:

> All pupils in the UK have to do PE, or Physical Education, at school until they are 16. The sports you can do at school depend on your school as each one offers different activities. The most popular sport at school is football, played by girls and boys.[1]

With the focus on mental health and well-being in recent years, a wider range of sports and activities are now available, for example the inclusion of yoga, pilates and dance. Students can also study PE as one of their GCSE and A-level subjects, but this is entirely dependent on staff being available to teach this and on the school itself promoting the course as a legitimate choice for young people at this stage of their learning. The idea that PE is a non-academic subject is reductive and does a disservice to the knowledge and learning opportunities afforded through the subject. Topics studied cover the theoretical and practical, enabling the development foundational study skills applicable to further learning and a wide range of other subjects.

On average, 14–16-year-olds do about 100 minutes of sport a week at school, but this reduces to 30 minutes a week for 17- and 18-year-olds.[2] It is easy to think that sports would somehow level the playing field, given that it is available to all from the very first year of secondary school. Yet, it is important to remember the additional cost of sports clothing and equipment, the availability of parents and carers to support before and/or after school, and the quality of provision available with schools themselves. These factors build on societal inequalities, exacerbating them within the school context.

A Department for Education report on PE in schools cited the following:

The PE and Sport Survey[3] found that:
- Schools where a high percentage of pupils took part in three or more hours of PE and out of hours school sport were more likely to be categorised as having low numbers of pupils on free school meals (FSM).
- Schools in deprived areas were over-represented amongst the lowest performing schools in terms of their participation in PE and out of hours school sport.
- Schools achieving the lowest levels of participation in three hours of PE and out of hours school sport tended to have a relatively high proportion of children from an ethnic minority background and pupils with special educational needs (SEN).

PERIOD 4: SPORTS

- Across all year groups boys were more likely to take part in three hours of PE and out of hours school sport than girls.[4]

The results of this survey offer some key points for reflection. First, there appears to be a correlation between FSM numbers and participation in school sport. In schools with lower numbers of children on FSM, more students take part in more sport. This is not difficult to understand, because of the aforementioned multiple challenges that children living with socio-economic disadvantage face. You can't play football or netball if you are constantly hungry or wondering whether you can attend practice or matches, or if you worry about actually having the sports clothing, and the ability to wash your sports kit so that you can play more than once a week. Second, schools in more affluent areas offer more PE within school and sport out of school. This may be down to a range of factors, including resourcing and space. Third, if you are a student from a minority ethnic background or with special education needs you are likely to do less sport – the report suggests this is a result of school provision and participation. Last, boys do more sports in and out of school compared to girls.

There is no doubt that the Covid-19 pandemic has had a colossal impact on sports in and beyond school, with the closing of schools and community facilities:

> A survey by the leading charity the Youth Sport Trust found 78% of parents said their children were doing less than the government's recommended 60 minutes of activity a day, while 11% of parents said their children are doing no physical activity at all. The total who said the amount had decreased in the past year was 68%, while only 15% said it had stayed the same.
>
> The research, conducted by YouGov among 1,109 parents, came as concerns continue to grow over the amount of sports provision available to children.[5]

The valiant efforts of sports enthusiasts, fitness professionals and former athletes to encourage children and young people to stay active during the pandemic has been both imaginative and laudable. But this does not replace the need for PE and sports activities in and beyond school. As if to pre-empt the survey, the government recognized that more needs to be done and for far more children and young people, to address the lack of provision that existed before the pandemic, but which inevitably was brought under the microscope of Covid-19.

> The Department of Education announced that £10m to 'encourage pupils to be more physically active' would be included as part of a £1bn programme of school building.
>
> The funding will be distributed by Sport England through its Active Partnerships county-level networks, which will work with local schools to identify those most in need.
>
> The government provides £320m to primary schools for sporting provision under its 'PE premium', a figure that was only confirmed for the current school year last July. The £10m is additional to that sum but will not only be expected to help disadvantaged pupils but increase accessibility to sports for disabled children and improve facilities, including swimming pools.[6]

The matter will not go away because the physical health of our children and young people depends on quality provision, qualified staff, and quantifiable spaces open and accessible to all, regardless of school or community location.

Spaces for sport

It is very easy to assume that every school has a playground. The quality of that playground and its suitability for the children of the school is a different question. To my knowledge, there is no national audit of playgrounds and sports spaces across English schools. The playground, which may be prime real estate in

PERIOD 4: SPORTS

some schools within certain areas of the country, is basic provision and needs to be protected so children can have some outdoor space in which to play.

A step up [from the playground] is the Multi Use Games Area, or MUGA, with its rubber crumb surface. Popular targets for investment today at both primary and secondary schools it enables sports that rely on a flat playing surface such as tennis or hockey.

The third major school sports facility to consider [after the multi-purpose school hall/ designated sports hall/ and playground/MUGA] is the swimming pool. It's a requirement for primary pupils to have swimming lessons as part of the curriculum. So, every school makes use of a swimming facility, be it proprietary or community based.

Nearly 40% of independent senior schools have their own pool. The number is closer to 12% for state secondary schools. At the primary level it's 33% for preps and around 3% for state.

But there are swimming pools and there are swimming pools. At the primary level one in five pools is outdoor. Which is fine for a summer splash when the sun comes out. But not that useful as a year-round water-sports enabling facility.[7]

This notion of space is at the heart of flourishing, not only in the metaphorical sense, but here too in the physical. Are our schools fit for purpose? Do they offer the right spaces for twenty-first-century learning and child-centred education? Do the buildings and grounds of a school facilitate participation and agency and growth of the imagination and creativity? These questions go beyond the space afforded to PE and sports in general. They do, however, underline the importance of physical health and well-being not being siloed and divided from mental health and well-being.

In order to address the growing need to replace some of the crippling infrastructure in schools successive UK governments have turned to Private Finance Initiative (PFI) schemes, which were 'introduced to the UK under the John Major Government in the 1990s, with the first PFI project [Skye Bridge] tested in Scotland'.[8] It is important, too, to remember that Tony Blair's New Labour Government significantly expanded PFI as a convenient way of funding public infrastructure 'off balance sheet'.[9] PFI schemes have been controversial, because 'for some it has come at a high price, leaving a legacy of unsustainable debt'. The problem here is that schools have relatively little say in the administration of the scheme, its impact and being able to assess whether it offers value for money:

> The Association of School and College Leaders (ASCL) has found that some schools are paying as much as 14 per cent of their funding each year to cover the costs of these deals. This is a particular problem in a time of real-terms budget cuts.
> So what are they paying for? In a nutshell, private sector providers build and operate the school infrastructure and provide facilities management services, such as cleaning, maintenance and security, for the length of the contract – usually 25 to 30 years.
> The school is not party to the contract; it exists between the local authority and the PFI contractor. The authority is responsible for managing and enforcing the contract, but there is a cost to schools of training staff to monitor service provision.
> The authority pays a fixed monthly charge for the capital investment, facilities management and any IT services provided. Schools contribute to this charge, as well as to the costs of any additional work undertaken by the facilities management provider.
> The monthly fixed-charge rises with inflation, and additional works are usually subject to a management fee, which could be up to 15 per cent of the cost of the work.[10]

The result in some cases is that school infrastructure is built as it is for adults not for children and young people. The buildings of many schools seem to be constructed around the idea

PERIOD 4: SPORTS

that children must be controlled otherwise 'all hell will break loose'. Some schools feel more like prisons in which young people are funnelled down corridors and controlled by bells. The subtle drive behind this architectural conceptualization is that human management is more important and less dangerous than human flourishing. All this has an impact of creating an oppressive and limiting atmosphere. I often wonder how many parents and carers would survive the daily routine of their children and young people without rebelling or questioning if things could be better.

The absence of the school voice in the management of the PFI scheme has long-term consequences for the educational provision of our children and young people:

> The central 'disconnect' in PFI is that the contract is not with the end user (i.e., the school) but with the local authority. In other words, the school does not have a direct 'voice'. How vigorously local authorities police these contracts is variable, and the situation is becoming more complex as their role shrinks.[11]

While some schools may be happy with the result of their PFI scheme, others are trapped in a cycle of debt and poor services and infrastructure. Both teachers and students suffer as there is very little that they can do to change the circumstances in which the school now finds itself. The lived experienced of those who have to endure the below standard services, buildings and spaces has yet to be fully researched.

In 2004, Tony Blair announced the 'Building Schools for the Future' initiative:

> Dubbed the biggest school building programme since Victorian times, Building Schools for the Future was Labour's £55bn grand plan to rebuild every secondary school in England.
>
> Announced by Tony Blair in 2004, the programme was about much more than replacing classrooms with leaking

roofs or buildings with crumbling brickwork. It was about initiating a step-change in children's education.

Not only were pupils to be provided with inspirational buildings that made them feel valued and worthwhile, but they were to be given access to new ways of learning fit for the 21st century.

This involved state of the art computer technology and, as such, required a change from the lay-out of a traditional school.

Instead of sitting in a class, filled with a line of wooden desks facing a teacher firmly ensconced in front of a chalk board, they might perch in wi-fi-enabled 'learning hubs', using their own laptops to carry out their own independent research.

And for the multi-billion-pound investment to be sustainable, the new facilities had to be flexible, as no one could predict what education would be like 50 years ahead.[12]

Just six years later, this programme was scrapped by Michael Gove under the Coalition Government (2010–15). Indeed, 'when Mr Gove axed the scheme, about 150 school projects were left in limbo, with a decision still to be made on whether they would proceed' and 'in the end, some 75 of these schools, mostly academies, were told their developments would go ahead'.[13] The ability to participate in, enjoy and flourish in sports at school and beyond has a lot to do with whether the existing equalities relating to the physical space and resources (teachers, equipment, sports clothing) are adequately addressed. We all want national, European, Commonwealth, World and Olympic champions who can inspire and motivate the next generation. My suspicion is that the United Kingdom is filled with these potential future sportspeople. They just may not be able to access and take part in the sports in which their talents can be fully realized.

Space matters. Space really matters. It matters who constructs it and how this is done. It matters how it is designated for a purpose and what it is called. The construction of the Helsinki

Central Library *Oodi*, for example, involved a consultative process from design to delivery with the local community and a wide range of users.[14] Researchers into school architecture cite examples across the world in which the children and young people have been involved in designing their school environment to match their needs, as well as those of their teachers:

> The inclusion of children in the design and planning process is also increasingly being encouraged.[15] The input of pupils has been claimed to have a positive impact on innovative design and in overcoming adult conservatism.[16] [As Chiles notes][17] The consultation process is portrayed as creative and educational for the pupils.[18]

Teachers and learners are trained in how to use these co-created spaces and investment is made into ensuring that spaces are dynamic and responsive. The work does not end with construction. It is important to see schools as a living, breathing places, not factories or prisons, or places where children and young people go to become less of who they are:

> The school setting is a complex environment that needs to mature. Post-occupancy evaluation processes and user feedback are therefore important complements to front-end user participation in design, as they facilitate an understanding of user needs and how the spaces are used in practice.[19]

Ultimately, if we want to give this gift of play, fun and health and well-being back to our children and young people, we need to be serious about PE and sports in our schools, ensuring that equal provision is facilitated at a local and national level.

Reimagining PE and sports

Let us imagine schools built with the depth and breadth of human imagination, built for good, for safety, for wholeness, for health and well-being, for healing. For some children and young people, PE and sport may be a crucial escape from unsafe homes. We need to redesign many of our schools to reflect spaces that become places for children and young people, imbued and shaped with meaning that engenders a sense of positive understanding of self, and takes dignity as the norm.

If we considered PE and sports as crucial to learning about self and body and mind, that these

> ... underlying learning intentions and values of the schools can be successfully incorporated into, and supported by, design. It means bringing these issues to the forefront of the discussion and ensuring that adequate investments are made in the early stages of the process in the form of time and resources.[20]

At the centre of the school could be spaces for play and gathering, PE and sports, spaces that were inclusive for, and enabled, all abilities and gifts to participate and enjoy the experience. Schools need to be connected to the communities in which they exist and not be isolated. Thus. the spaces available in the community for sports activities need to be made accessible to children and young people at no extra cost. The wealthiest sports clubs and companies could build and sustainably fund community facilities, ring-fencing access to these facilities all year round for children and young people. In all of this, the welfare and safety of children and young people would be paramount. Sports activities would not need to be limited to the school day. Rather, with a reimagined school day and school year, learning and participating in sports could be a year-long journey of discovery.

Resourcing the professional teaching of PE and sports in schools should be funded by government and national sporting bodies. If we want more home-grown Wimbledon champions, then the LTA should build local tennis courts and a sporting company or club should fund the provision of equipment and free coaching across communities in the UK. There should be an integrated programme that encourages physical and mental health and well-being between school and community, showing children and young people how to develop their learning and sporting interests all year long. It feels like the successive governments we have had to date simply do not care enough about children and young people to develop the holistic approach needed for a child to flourish in PE and sport. We need to reimagine this subject not as a subject but as a way of life facilitated in and beyond school.

Notes

1 British Council, 'Sport at School', *British Council*, https://learnenglishteens.britishcouncil.org/uk-now/read-uk/sport-school, accessed 28.02.2022.
2 British Council, 'Sport at School'.
3 Susannah Quick, Aline Simon and Alex Thornton, Department for Education, *PE and sport survey 2009/10*, TNS-BMRB, 2010, DFE RR032.
4 Department for Education, 2013, *Evidence on physical education and sport in schools*, www.gov.uk/government/publications/evidence-on-physical-education-and-sport-in-schools, pp. 3–4, accessed 31.05.2021.
5 Paul MacInnes, 2021, 'Survey shows UK parents' concern over Covid effect on children's activity', *The Guardian*, 5 March, www.theguardian.com/sport/2021/mar/05/survey-shows-uk-parents-concern-over-covid-effect-on-childrens-activity, accessed 28.02.2022.
6 MacInnes, 2021, 'English schools to get extra £10m to open sports facilities after hours', *The Guardian*, 5 February, www.theguardian.com/education/2021/feb/05/english-schools-to-get-extra-10m-to-open-sports-facilities-after-hours, accessed 28.02.2022.
7 Schoolsmith, 2019, 'School sports facilities; how do they vary?', 12 June, *Schoolsmith*, www.schoolsmith.co.uk/school-sports-facilities/, accessed 28.02.2022.
8 Joel Benjamin, 2014, 'Seven things everyone should know about the Private Finance Initiative', 17 November, *Open Democracy*, www.opendemocracy.net/en/ournhs/seven-things-everyone-should-know-about-private-finance-initiative/, accessed 28.02.2022.
9 Benjamin, 'Seven things everyone should know about the Private Finance Initiative'.

10 Julia Harnden, 2016, 'PFI must not be put into the "too difficult" drawer', *Schools Week*, 11 July, https://schoolsweek.co.uk/pfi-must-not-be-put-into-the-too-difficult-drawer/, accessed 28.02.2022.

11 Harnden, 'PFI must not be put into the "too difficult" drawer'.

12 BBC, 2011, 'Q&A: Building Schools for the Future', 14 June, *BBC News*, www.bbc.co.uk/news/education-10682980, accessed 28.02.2022.

13 BBC, 'Q&A: Building Schools for the Future'.

14 Oodi, Helsinki, 'Service Design', www.oodihelsinki.fi/en/what-is-oodi/service-design/, accessed 16.05.2022.

15 Mark Francis and Ray Lorenzo, 2002, 'Seven realms of children's participation', *Journal of Environmental Psychology*, 22(1–2), pp. 157–69.

16 Leanne Rivlin and Maxine Wolfe, 1985, *Institutional Settings in Children's Lives*, New York: Wiley.

17 Prue Chiles, 2003, 'Classrooms for the future: an adventure in design and research' in *Architectural Research Quarterly*, 7(3–4), pp. 244–60.

18 Roine Leiringer and Paula Cardellino, 2011, 'Schools for the twenty-first century: school design and educational transformation', *British Educational Research Journal*, 37(6), pp. 915–34, p. 920.

19 Leiringer and Cardellino, 'Schools for the twenty-first century', p. 930.

20 Leiringer and Cardellino, 'Schools for the twenty-first century', p. 931.

Period 5: Science

Universal Matter

O Lord, our Sovereign,
how majestic is your name in all the earth!

You have set your glory above the heavens.
Out of the mouths of babes and infants
you have founded a bulwark because of your foes,
to silence the enemy and the avenger.

When I look at your heavens, the work of your fingers,
the moon and the stars that you have established;
what are human beings that you are mindful of them,
mortals that you care for them?

Yet you have made them a little lower than God,
and crowned them with glory and honour.
You have given them dominion over the works of your
    hands;
you have put all things under their feet,
all sheep and oxen,
and also the beasts of the field,
the birds of the air, and the fish of the sea,
whatever passes along the paths of the seas.

O Lord, our Sovereign,
how majestic is your name in all the earth!
(Psalm 8)

There is a glorious expression of life in creation and in the world beneath our feet and above our heads. The disciplines of earth science, chemistry, physics, maths and biology, and the related sciences, give insight into the heavens and the earth.

We are part of both and are accountable to both. Despite our human ingenuity, there is much in the universe we did not and cannot create. We cannot create the moon or stars, nor can we ever fully claim to create human beings. We understand the science behind our lives and breath, but we are yet to take responsibility for what that science is telling us about how we should live and what we should remember about our fragile selves and world.

In all of this, we laud our human existence over creation, as if we are not part of it, and misuse the words of the Hebrew Bible to affirm our claimed superiority. Yet, we exist only because of the love and grace of the divine, also given and emitted through others to help us uphold our individual and collective lives. Our mortality can frighten us into thinking that this is all there is, this world, this time, this place, this domination. The truth is we are creatures, like others on our planet, and we are still to learn the lesson of peaceful co-existence and respectful care of our earthly home. We have great power, but we do not have great wisdom as a human race.

The word 'dominion' is a poor translation of the psalm. If we feel such power over the animal kingdom of which we are a part, how much more power will some feel over fellow human beings? If we think of the root word 'domus', meaning house, would we trash, pollute, strip down and almost destroy a house we had been given and in which we were requested to live? The science of being a custodian is built on the equation of tender care, foresight and service. The earth, the air and the sea were made for all, and were never meant to be commodified. The bounty of the field, the air and sea are sufficient for us as a human race, if we did not convince ourselves that some deserved more of this bounty than others. The most dangerous science is the one that presents the human need for hierarchy and categorization as objective fact, and claims that this home we call earth was meant only for some and not for all. This is not science, but a lie.

* * *

PERIOD 5: SCIENCE

Why didn't anyone tell us? Why didn't anyone tell us that the science we were learning in the classroom, in the lab, with our Bunsen burners, beakers, and wooden worktops, was all around us? In the great trees that lined our playground, in our physiology, in our proudly produced recipes in home economics, and our journeys through the city by bus or by foot to school. Our science teachers did the best with what they had, but my memory of science is that it was so confined to the classroom and/or lab and bore little relation to the outside world. I enjoyed science at school but was encouraged to take the 'double award', which gave me two GCSEs. The double award or combined science was introduced in the 1990s. In my current role as Head of Education at a livery company and of its charity that focuses on supporting and promoting chemistry and related sciences (the Salters' Institute), I wonder what on earth my teachers would say, after picking up their jaws from the floor.

At our girls' school we all did science as stipulated by the National Curriculum. There was no question that we could not study science or that we could not perform brilliantly in the subject. There were only two options for us to choose from: the double or the triple award, the latter separating out the sciences into single subjects (biology, chemistry, physics). I was not inspired by science in school, despite the female science teachers throughout my school career. I was not brought into the magnificence and majesty of the material world; this was a great opportunity missed. Now, as an adult, my fascination has been rekindled through my work, and through engagement with chemists, engineers, science educators, technicians and innovators. Now I can see what I was not told, the connections that were not clearly spelled out to me and the need for a better understanding of our world and ourselves within it.

Science in schools

Science has been designated a core subject of the National Curriculum, alongside mathematics and English, since the Education Reform Act of 1988 (Ofsted, April 2021).[1] Yet what does science mean for the child or young person in the classroom? How does that differ, if at all, to the reality of how a particular discipline is used beyond the classroom? How does the curriculum speak to the movements and calls of the age? Because science always does. It always speaks to what is and is not happening in society, and it responds scientifically. Our responsibility to children and young people is that we enable and prepare them to understand and interact with science and, if they wish, continue with the subject into adulthood, embracing it not only for career purposes but as part of a commitment to lifelong learning. For the Campaign for Science and Engineering (CaSE), the UK's leading independent advocate for science and engineering, 'a broad and balanced science education is not only important to encourage more children to become scientists and engineers but also to increase the science capital of the next generation'.[2]

Without going into the intricacies of the curriculum for each of the three sciences (biology, chemistry and physics), we know that:

> In England, science is assessed at key stage 4 (aged 15–16) as either combined science worth 2 GCSE grades, or as 3 separate science GCSEs, commonly referred to as triple science. A minority of pupils complete entry level or vocational qualifications. At key stage 5 (aged 16–18), pupils can choose to study A levels in the 3 sciences, as well as environmental science. There is also a range of vocational science qualifications. Health and science T levels begin in autumn 2021.[3]

This picture does not tell you that the combined science is by far the more prevalent option for students in secondary schools. According to the Wellcome Trust's survey of young people in 2019:

> Most year 10–13 students said their school offered triple science as part of the school curriculum. However, not all of these students were given the opportunity to study it. Barriers to studying triple science appear to have been more related to the school being selective in who studies it, rather than not offering it at all. Barriers to uptake of triple science were mainly personal factors such as confidence and lack of interest, although some were discouraged by not meeting grade thresholds or by their teacher.[4]

It is clear that the triple science option has more content and may be more challenging. No good and committed teacher would ever wish to set up their learners for a fall. Yet when schools are trying to play the league table game to ensure that only their best students have the chance to study triple science, then we have a serious problem, and especially if these decisions lead to demographic exclusion from science subjects. The provision of triple science is often linked to socio-economic advantage and schools where it can be offered. You are more likely to continue with a science to A level if you have studied triple science. Further, some schools do not allow students to progress to A level in a science if they have not studied triple science. So, if we have a school that limits the access to triple science as a GCSE choice, this shuts a big door in terms of options for future studies in the sciences, and ultimately of career pathways.

The departure point, from where a student starts their engagement with science, does not determine their long-term relationship with the subject:

> Students from more disadvantaged backgrounds (as measured by free school meals eligibility and area deprivation level) were no less interested in science and were as likely as more advantaged students to aspire to a STEM pathway in

post-16 subject choices and in a career. Among those considering higher education, students from less advantaged backgrounds were also as likely as other students to consider a STEM pathway (although from year 10 they were less likely to aspire to university in general).[5]

How do we translate this interest and curiosity into an engagement with the subject in school and beyond, with possible careers in STEM as young adults? In its 2021 report, 'Inspiring Innovation', CaSE offers three key recommendations for improving and maintaining science education:

1. A confident and empowered teaching workforce
2. Making science and engineering careers inclusive to all young people
3. Exploration of innovation through practical, hands-on science.[6]

Reading this backwards we could assume, therefore, that the current teaching workforce lacks confidence and has been disempowered through curricula interventions and cuts; careers in science and engineering are not yet as inclusive as they could be; and that there is an issue with the provision of practical science in schools. All of these elements would clearly disrupt the path to flourishing in this subject. The reality is that teachers matter, and their role in inspiring as well as enhancing and building motivation cannot be underestimated. Further, schools in socio-economically challenging areas struggle to recruit qualified and good teachers:

> The Sutton Trust, in a survey of 3,000 teachers, showed that a more comprehensive set of measures, including reduced timetables, offer of a substantial promotion and the opportunity to work with a talented teacher who they could learn from would be attractive for teachers to work in an educationally disengaged community.[7]

PERIOD 5: SCIENCE

We know, too, that science is not as diverse as it could be. Children and young people do not necessarily see themselves represented across the disciplines. There is also under-representation for people with disabilities, women and Black and global majority heritage peoples in senior roles within the scientific workforce.[8] According to a report by the Royal Society in 2014,[9] women are also under-represented in certain first-degree subjects.

The challenge is not just limited to teachers, but also incorporates the people who will prepare and assist with the practical work: technicians. Ofsted confirms that 'technicians provide a crucial role in supporting high-quality practical work in schools'. However, research shows that not all schools have enough science technicians. Indeed, 'schools in areas of higher social deprivation tend to be worst affected'.[10] This is further corroborated by CaSE. Citing a 2016 survey,[11] it notes that:

> 72% of school technicians were over the age of 40, meaning that the majority of science technicians will be set to leave the profession in the next 20 years. The survey also highlights concerns in attracting people to the profession if the role is undervalued and continues to offer little career progression, with two-thirds of the then technician workforce feeling there were no opportunities for development. The average number of FTE science technicians per school has fallen by 16 per cent since 2011/12. Additionally, schools with a less affluent pupil intake tend to have less technician support than those with a more affluent intake. Failure to attract and retain technicians, threatens the availability and quality of practical science in schools.[12]

We have, therefore, a situation in which some schools offer triple science, and some do not. Other schools select who is then able to do triple science at GCSE. Some schools also do not have enough teachers or technicians. In all of this, it is the child or young person that pays the price as they suffer the consequences: the reduction in their options and a lack of teaching staff and technicians. More needs to be done to empower and enable educators to teach the subject they love and to which they are committed. Further, there needs to be more research into the impact of options taken in schools on later subject studies and career and educational pathways. Last, it is also important to establish and interrogate the data on which schools and students are offered and then allowed to study triple science (or their equivalent) across the home nations.

The impact of the pandemic on science teaching has been significant across different areas. According to the Medical Schools Council, for example, 'the total number of applications for medicine at UK universities for entry in 2021 is 28,690, up 20.9% compared to applications for entry in 2020'.[13] Entry to one of the most competitive degrees had become even more so. There was also 'a 34% increase in applications to nursing courses in England' (UCAS, February 2021), with UCAS receiving '48,830 applications to nursing courses in England, up from 35,960 at the same point in 2020'.[14] Covid-19 has brought science to the fore in the minds of all and into the public consciousness like never before. The pandemic has inspired children and young people to pursue a career and path that speaks to this increased awareness, a career they feel has purpose that addresses immediate and future need, and possible science literacy.

Historical debate

In a letter to the scientific journal *Nature* in 1988, a member of the public wrote to express their outrage and concern at the new method for science teaching in schools. Too long to cite here, the abridged version, nonetheless, highlights some of the key issues within the historical debate and what should be taught and how this content should be delivered:

PERIOD 5: SCIENCE

SIR

Science teachers in Britain are being pressed to introduce changes that pose a serious threat to standards, especially for pupils of high academic ability. I refer to what is variously called 'integrated science', 'balanced science', or simply 'science'...

Two features of the proposals give reason for disquiet. The first is that integrated science will take up at most two subjects in the GCSE curriculum. Pupils who at present take physics and chemistry separately will therefore be presented with a diluted version of those subjects because one-third less time will be allotted; further dilution will occur because the syllabus is necessarily aimed at pupils who have considerably less ability to handle mathematical topics.

The second source of anxiety is the pressure upon specialist teachers of physics, chemistry and biology to teach outside their own specialities. Is it an appropriate use of scarce manpower for physicists to labour over the microscopy of living cells, or for biologists to struggle with the concept of valency? What will the consequences be for recruitment if science teachers are to be prevented from teaching what they know and enjoy and understand best? And have the implications for safety in school science laboratories received any attention from the reformers? A knock-on effect upon university standards appears to be inevitable. Advanced-level physical science syllabuses are already being down-graded to take account of the change from O-level to GCSE; if a majority of pupils take two-subject 'science', further downward revision can be confidently predicted.[15]

I think there is something in this letter that still resonates in more modern discussions about secondary school science. Standards and quality of teaching and learning continue to be debated. What teachers actually teach, and how this aligns with their academic and pedagogical training, is an ongoing challenge. The reality is, owing to the shortage of qualified teachers in specific disciplines, teachers are asked to teach subjects that they did not study at degree level. This is where the division between specialist and non-specialist educators can be clearly seen. A science teacher and chemistry teacher, for example, may have had similar educational pathways but different opportunities to access and attend subject-specific-training. It will be important to assess this demanding context and its impact on teaching and learning, and on if and how the student is able to create cross-curricular connections.

What to teach

The content of science teaching, and how we measure its quality, has had an international profile in recent decades. In 2012, the National Research Council in the US devised their new framework and standards for teaching science: *A Framework for K-12 Science Education Practices, Crosscutting Concepts, and Core Ideas*.[16] It is impressive in its breadth and its presentation of what science is. Taking a much broader approach to secondary science, its core concepts have the aim of being scientifically literate. There are:

- 8 science and engineering practices (knowledge and skills)
- 7 crosscutting concepts (fundamental concepts that bridge ideas)
- 44 disciplinary core ideas (content and the idea of progression)
  - Physical sciences
  - Life sciences
  - Earth and space sciences
  - Engineering, technology and applications of science

The framework also presents this idea stated above of three-dimensional learning to enable and promote children's and young people's understanding of phenomena in their environment. There is an emphasis on contextual teaching and learning, and a move away from the siloed presentation of the three sciences. What is particularly interesting is that the sciences not taught at secondary level, earth sciences and engineering for example, are brought into the secondary space, thus promoting not only the theoretical but applied learning and practical application.

Of course, the US is a different context. Yet, textbooks and worksheets cannot be the only source of learning or from which enquiry occurs. The child and young person's local context, social and environmental milieu all have a part to play in how they approach the learning and appreciation of science. Since the launch of the Next Generation Science Standards in the US, the three institutions (The Royal Society of Biology, The Royal Society of Chemistry, and the Institute of Physics) have responded by devising their own frameworks for the UK context. Yet it is important to note that the existence of the three separate institutions does not match the science taught in a unified form in most schools.

There are also the knock-on effects of the pandemic on practical science, which cannot be ignored:

> A 2020 report from the Association for Science Education[17] surveyed science teachers and science technicians looking at how schools have responded to the challenges posed by virtual learning and social distancing in schools ... Almost 60% of respondents (both science leaders and teachers) were not satisfied with their school or college provision for practical work during lockdown. Schools and colleges anticipated a big reduction in the frequency of practical science taught from September 2020, with respondents estimating it was likely that 20% of GCSE and A level classes would have no practical science at all. In addition to the logistical challenges of carrying out practical science during the pandemic, nearly 90% of respondents were concerned about the pressure to catch up on missed content during the first lockdown period from March 2020, with likely knock-on effects on the amount of time that would be spent on activities such as practical work and classroom discussion. The ASE have

made a number of recommendations for how schools can amend their practices in order to still meet the Gatsby Good Practical Science benchmarks.[18]

The challenge of having little to no practical science, and especially for those aged 14–18, means that the preparation needed for the next stage of their learning is severely hampered. The progression from GCSE to A level or A level to university without the practical core skills leaves all learners at a disadvantage and struggling to cope with and access future learning without the fundamental practice and familiarity with practical science. Children and young people who have had access to better resources and facilities will have an advantage as they progress through to the next stage of their education.

In 1998, Robin Millar and Jonathan Osborne wrote:

> School science, particularly at secondary level, fails to sustain and develop the sense of wonder and curiosity of many young people about the natural world. This interest and inquisitiveness which characterises many primary school children's response to science diminishes at secondary level to a degree which cannot wholly be accounted for by the onset of adolescence. The apparent lack of relevance of the school science curriculum to teenagers' curiosity and interests contributes to too few young people choosing to pursue solely courses in science and mathematics post-16, preferring instead to follow either courses in the humanities or a mixed combination drawn from a range of disciplines.[19]

I wonder how far we have come from these initial statements and what still needs responding to. Reports are published almost every year on secondary science and more will be published still, all of which will need to respond to old and new challenges of the twenty-first century. In my view, these challenges are: how we live with finite resources, how we deal with global health and maladies, how we understand what it is to be human in the face of technological advancement, and how we

PERIOD 5: SCIENCE

redefine our relationship with the natural world through a lens of interdependence not subjugation. There is also something in Millar and Osborne's words about the purpose and legacy of science education at secondary level, which has shifted over time and continues to do so, whether the emphasis is on the creation of scientists, engineers, inventors and innovations or all or none of these. Behind purpose and legacy must rest an ethical framework and underpinning that seeks to affirm our common humanity, aims to interrogate and examine for the benefit of humanity, that improves communities not at the cost of the erasure or disenfranchisement of others, and explores our purpose-filled place within a complex and majestic cosmos.

Reimagining science

What if we had a new body for the secondary sector whose focus was scientific interdisciplinary learning across the home nations? Their role would be to develop a new way of integrating environmental and earth science, materials science, engineering and interdisciplinary approaches to science at the secondary level. Why are these subjects only introduced at degree level, when some elements of each can be taught before this stage? The body would comprise more women than men and would be more representative of society and its diversity across ethnicity, religion, beliefs and identities.

How can we better connect science to the local contexts and lived experiences of children and young people? We could dismantle the current assessment processes with its focus on exams and incorporate more practical work and contextual teaching and learning. Laboratories that are well equipped and easily accessible have to be available for every school. And can laboratories be decoupled from schools? Could empty undergraduate university labs be used for local community projects in the summer vacation? Elevating and protecting the role of the science technician while affirming the role of the classroom teacher should not be mutually exclusive. Could we create a new national association for science technicians that emphasized career and educational paths and advocated better working conditions and pay for this essential workforce? Ultimately, science has to be brought alive to build on the curiosity and inquisitive minds of children and young people. To do this science has to be brought to the community level, from which local and future leaders, thinkers and innovators will emerge.

Notes

1 Ofsted, 2021, *Research review series: science*, 29 April, *Gov.uk*, www.gov.uk/government/publications/research-review-series-science/research-review-series-science, accessed 01.03.2022.
2 Campaign for Science and Engineering (CaSE), 2021, *Inspiring Innovation*, July, p. 2.
3 Ofsted, *Research review series: science*.
4 Wellcome Trust, 2020, *Young People's Views on Science Education, Science Education Tracker 2019* (Wave 2), p. 8.
5 Wellcome Trust, p. 10.
6 CaSE, *Inspiring Innovation*, p. 3.
7 CaSE, *Inspiring Innovation*, p. 5.
8 This is defined by the Royal Society as 'all those for whom their scientific knowledge, training, and skills are necessary for the work that they do'. The Royal Society, 2014, *A picture of the UK scientific workforce. Diversity data analysis for the Royal Society – Summary Report*, p. 3.
9 The Royal Society, 2014, *A picture of the UK scientific workforce. Diversity data analysis for the Royal Society – Summary Report*, p. 5.
10 Ofsted, *Research review series: science*.
11 Preproom.org, 2016, *UK School Science Technician Survey*.
12 CaSE, *Inspiring Innovation*, p. 11.
13 Medical Schools Council, 2021, 'Record number of applicants to medicine results in increased competition for places', 23 February, *Medical Schools Council*, www.medschools.ac.uk/news/record-number-of-applicants-to-medicine-results-in-increased-competition-for-places, accessed 01.03.2022.
14 Department of Health and Social Care, 'Nursing applications in England up by over a third to 48,830', *Gov.uk*, www.gov.uk/

government/news/nursing-applications-in-england-up-by-over-a-third-to-48830, accessed 01.03.2022.

15 Letter to *Nature* Vol. 333(5), May 1988, p 9.

16 National Research Council, 2012, *A Framework for K-12 Science Education: Practices, Crosscutting Concepts, and Core Ideas*, Washington, DC: The National Academies Press.

17 The Association for Science Education, 2020, *Good Practical Science - making it happen post-Covid-19*.

18 Campaign for Science and Engineering (CaSE), *Inspiring Innovation*, p. 11.

19 Robin Millar and Jonathan Osborne, 1998, *Beyond 2000: Science Education for the Future*, London: King's College London, p. 3.

INTERVIEW WITH PROFESSOR CHRIS JACKSON, CHAIR IN SUSTAINABLE GEOSCIENCE, UNIVERSITY OF MANCHESTER

22 April 2021

CJ: I was born and raised in Derby, which is a very industrial, working-class small city in the East Midlands, in a predominantly white neighbourhood in that city. The school I was in was not racially and ethnically mixed. I guess there were two kinds of main groups: there were white students, who were in the dominant group and then there were quite a lot of South Asian students, Bangladeshi, Pakistani, Indian, or first generation born in the UK at that time in the 1980s. There were probably six Black kids in my year of around 230. So, it was a large secondary comprehensive school.

During that time, I guess I had a pretty good time of it really. I was academically able. I had parents who were not academically educated beyond the age of 15 in the Caribbean, but they valued education sufficiently that they let me kind of get on with it. So, they didn't devalue education by saying, 'This is all a waste of time. You should go and get a real job' sort of communication. Neither did they then have the other kind of Caribbean experience I've heard of, or kind of some 'African experiences', I've heard of where the parents are very, very forceful. They weren't dismissive of education, nor were they particularly overbearing around it and that kind of suits my personality to have freedom of choice about how much I engage.

INTERVIEW

At that time, I guess, I kind of developed another persona which was very much around sport, and I was always quite outgoing personally, and sporty. I guess that I was forced to fit in, in a way, and become popular in a different way at school by just being engaged in all the other stuff people were engaged in. Now I don't know if that was conscious moulding. And I don't think that it was. It was just that was what I was interested in. I'd have run with the white kids who were on my street or in my class, because they were really good friends, and still are.

I think that was overall my experience then in terms of the general experience. In terms of specific lowlights, they were kind of few and far between. There were racially motivated incidents or negative incidents, where name calling is, I guess you'd call it standard, but it's kind of horrible to say that, you know. There was that. And there were a few incidents with teachers at school where, in all likelihood, was that there was a race element, where there was some profiling around: 'This incident happened. It's likely it was you because of this, because of the colour of your skin.' And again, like I said, those things were relatively few and far between. So, I don't have strong recollections of large amounts of racial abuse happening when I was at school. Undoubtedly, looking back though from my position now, there was a lot of what would be called micro-aggressions in today's language, where there were still names being called and trying to diminish somebody by referring to the colour of their skin. You know, there was also 'go back home' and a poor understanding of what nation states are, citizenship, diaspora. You know what all of those things mean [but] 13-, 14-, 15-year-olds don't really care about the fineries of that.

And highlights were just getting on with my life, just trying to achieve in the things that I was interested in. At that time, it was primarily sports: playing at quite a high level of football, doing a lot of athletics at national level, working hard. But I was never particularly a studious kid at all. I found enjoyment outside the classroom, outside school largely, although I was still sufficiently engaged in the educational experience to get value from it. Some people will look at Black people as being a homogeneous group. And there is a great amount of heterogeneity in there. People wonder about using the term BAME or people of colour. Even if you got down to the 'B' of BAME, within that 'B' there is a great diversity of experiences and personality types which then impact how incidents land and stay with you for your life, and shape who you are. So, if you're like me, who's a bit thick-skinned and gobby, 'resilient' would be the word in modern talk, then those things are a bit more water off a duck's back – although there is an accumulated stress or strain from those experiences. For some people one incident is enough to throw them off, like one brush with the police, for example. I have had a few brushes with the police. All the time I was innocent, but it didn't bother me because I knew I was right. I knew I was innocent and didn't give a crap really.

MIB: How then did somebody that wasn't particularly studious end up giving the [2020] Christmas Lecture at the Royal Institution?

CJ: I don't know. I don't think you have to be studious.

MIB: Was it just being driven, having determination and a love of subject?

CJ: No, it's loads of luck and chance, and support. I think this myth of 'if you work hard enough you will achieve' ... You often just need to encounter fewer barriers than somebody else. I think we've all got potential, but we don't all have opportunity. I think one way of explaining it is that, you know, there's probably lots of other Black Christmas lecturers out there, and there have been in the past and they've not had access to that opportunity because there have been barriers in their way, or they have not been fortunate enough to look into a network which then would allow them to be selected for that thing.

INTERVIEW

MIB: It's sort of like Michelle Obama's mother, Mrs Robinson, always saying: 'My kids aren't special. There are loads of Michelles and Craigs on the South Side.' There is a plethora of potential.

CJ: Exactly. Exactly. So, I think with the Christmas Lectures, it kind of speaks to the fact that you don't have to define yourself. And this I think is important for Black people. You don't need to define yourself by your subject and your science. You can still like rap music. You can still wear hoodies. You can still go and hang out on the corner or go to a cookout, or something ... You can still, if you wish, go and do that, still embed yourself in the culture of which you are most comfortable. You should still be able to do that and still have access to those opportunities. So, for me, I've never defined myself as a scientist or as being particularly studious because, quite frankly, you know there's loads of other things I like doing equally as much as like doing the job I do. I like being with my friends. I like being with my family. I like cycling and running. I love all those things and those things for me are as important a part of my character as being studious. I think that's important because what it does is opens up the market to a lot more people to achieve in an academic way, or attain something in an academic way. A degree, or PhD or whatever it is. It says you don't need to be this white middle-class person who has had all these opportunities, who reads clever books and listens to classical music, and you know has all of these things. Neither if you're Black, you don't need to realign yourself with that vision which is required to then advance on.

If you want to become an academic, there should be a range of different ways of achieving that, and if we recognize that then we are going to allow a broader set of people to have access to that opportunity.

MIB: It sounds like you're talking about what I would describe as this wholeness, that you come to education with your whole person and your whole self. And what happens with the education system is [that] it tries to funnel you into very specific routes and says, actually, it becomes quite binary. So, you can't be a scientist and also love art. You can't be an artist and tinker around as an amateur engineer. And I think that there is a challenge in that because young people, I don't think get the message that you can have plural interests, and plural affinities, actually.

CJ: Yes. I am just thinking as well that my wife is a teacher at primary school. I don't think that is a failing of the teachers as individuals. [Teachers] who say: 'Here's Jerome. He turns up like this, but has he got a spark for science. But we need to suppress that because unless he changes what he wears, and the music he listens to.' I don't think the individuals are doing that. I wonder if it is more systemic language. And it's one thing I am kind of interested in. I haven't done anything with it, but it always is at the back of my mind after my wife sort of talked to me a bit about it. How we educate people is done in a very like: 'There is a train going from London to Bradford. It's going 60mph, and now do this calculation.' And some kids, they're in central London or where I grew up in Derby going, 'I don't know where Bradford is!' So, you know, the reason for doing that calculation is without context particularly. Whereas it would be better saying, 'We're in school now. You're going to meet Colin or Sarah in the park, you know, the one just round the corner from the school and you're going to be walking at 2mph' and you actually contextualize, you bring the experience, the academic learning into a space which is more familiar to them, and perhaps more relevant, of course.

Let's take a horribly stereotyped one. So, you're looking at writing a song. It's two minutes long, your hip hop beats are going to have, like 40 beats per minute. And you know the beatboxing is going to be like 80 beats per minute. You can do something where you actually engage people. And I would say that's how I got into earth sciences. I was a s*** scientist. It was my second lowest GCSE grade was science, ahead of French. So I wasn't very good at science relative to some other subjects. And the reason that I got interested in science was more by just looking around in the landscapes and looking out into the wider world and being interested in why it looked like it did and then coming back to the physical underpinnings of why the earth looks like it does. It wasn't the other way around like, 'Well, here's all this maths and physics and chemistry which is a little bit abstract, and has been contextualized for you, Chris, with these examples that you don't really understand. You know, like, good luck!' It was actually the other way around. So, I am still not a particularly good classically-trained physical scientist by any stretch at all, but I am interested in those things, because I am interested in trying to understand something which is for me more tangible. I don't know if you call it kinaesthetic [learning], something where you can feel it and then there is a provocation to go and learn from that.

MIB: Have we got it right with secondary science education?

CB: I don't know. I am not in secondary science education. And I know my experience of it was sort of OK. It wasn't great. It was a bit abstract for me, like I said. Same with maths, which is why I got an A in maths and a D in science, but I dropped both of them for A level because it wasn't particularly clear to me why it would lead to a job, why it was interesting anyway in itself, even regardless of a job. Whether we've got it right or wrong, I don't know because I think there are education experts, pedagogic experts, and there are people who know a lot more about science and just general education at that level than me.

Some of the things I hear and read about are troubling in the academy system, for example. There are aspects of that which I find deeply troubling, just as a citizen. And I hate it when people go 'as a parent' because you don't need to be a parent to think that there are some aspects of our education system that are a bit crap. But it certainly makes me more aware ... So, with aspects of the academy system, focusing on not the whole self, but focusing on the classic disciplines because these are the things that Ofsted are coming to measure. [So, the thinking is]: 'Therefore, we need to curtail creativity and curtail, you know, spontaneous engagement in something because Ofsted are going to measure us in this or these middle-class parents are going to go to these league tables here. And the things that are driving those league tables are maths and English and science, so that's what we need to do.' I think that the bits that are worrying, bits of what we are seeing at the moment of education being caught up in the culture wars sort of thing. This whole Pimlico Academy thing,[1] which is still going on. This deep concern about the politicization of schools and, on the flipside, there is something incredibly invigorating about children walking out of school and laying so much on the line to defend what they believe in, you know. The right to wear a hairstyle, the right to wear a headscarf, the right to not have a flag outside the school because they are having this kind of culture impressed upon them. I think, in that respect, out of something as crappy as that experience, that conflict I find very invigorating and empowering.

MIB: I just wondered how you would define education, from your experience, or it can be from just thoughts that you have had throughout your professional life.

CJ: I think it comes down to this: there's one vision of what success would be and often it's money and power and influence. And then you work backwards from that. What do you need to get there? Well, you need an education. You need friends and networks and therefore instantly you're in a space where you have to be a certain racial group, or ethnic group. So, you kind of work back to there. And then you're saying the things that are most likely to achieve those things for you are these classically defined subjects. So we're going to define success for you. Success for you is going to be As in maths, physics, chemistry, biology, you know, but you can't be successful if you become a plumber. Or you can't be successful if you become a postal worker. Or if you become a healthcare worker, that's not success. That's lower down the food chain. You're going to be paid less. And I think what education needs to be about is making people *maximize their potential*, and so that people are working in those jobs. Even if they're being paid less than people working in some other jobs, they feel that they have fulfilled their potential and they are doing something with love and with care and with training that makes them feel confident in that job.

I have this discussion with my wife occasionally. You know GCSEs have this very set form. We force everybody up to the age of 16 and then they can choose to do A levels. By then many people are disenfranchised with education, because already they've 'failed' at this subset of things which we've selected as being things you need to know. And we give them options maybe at the age of 14 for GCSE, but by then it could be too late. There are other education systems like in Germany and in Denmark and some other places where you would say 'You're not academically good in this subject, so what we're going to do is we're going to train you and give you practical training in electrical engineering so that you could become an electrician, or we give you practical training in plumbing, or practical training in some aspect of civil engineering so you can work with infrastructure design and things.'

[Some would say] well, you're kind of saying these people aren't clever enough to do long division or integrations. I don't think it's that. I think it's saying that *we have* these people with different skills and interests. If we take them down [only] one path, then we're obviously going to have a binary there. We're going to have people who are going to make it through that system and people who aren't. And the people who aren't are not going to want to engage in education of *any* sort, potentially because their experience with education has been, you know, that they have been deemed a 'failure' because they have not been able to do this thing which for them, and for many people, they can't really see the value of.

But then there's this other clear job market or huge bit of the job market or the economy which requires people with skills in this area over here. We're not doing a good enough job, it seems, of maximizing the engagement and the training and the enjoyment that those people will have in those other areas. And again, I don't know enough about whether this works in all these different countries I've mentioned, but I do find it interesting that the thought that, OK, maybe at 15 (and who knows what they want at 15, is the argument my wife gives me back), but at 15 or 16 maybe, my argument was let's make education compulsory to 18. But then in the last two years from 16–18, which are classed as the A level years, then at 16 you can choose whether you want to go into something which is vocation ... you go and do whatever you wanted then. So that would be my argument about one way of reimagining what secondary education could look like. And it goes to your question about what is education vs programming?

MIB: I think it's really interesting because I am in the school of thought that talks about education linked to the flourishing of the whole person, and that *that* requires investment. And the problem with the education system we have is that it creates, it commodifies our young people. So, they are worth a certain amount to the school. They have to be funnelled through a system. The school gets funding based on the number of students it has and the school is judged based on the results of those young people. So, actually, there isn't room for the kind of career guidance and conversation that you have with a young person to explore their interest because the pressure is so much on them to choose who they are going to be really, really early. And I have had a lot of conversations with young people centred around shame. They're ashamed of their grades. They're ashamed that they are not doing what their parents want. They're ashamed that they're not going to be considered a success. They're ashamed that they've not chosen the right universities on their UCAS form. And that shame goes with you for a really long time ... And so you can imagine the layers and layers of narratives that young people carry and the education system, for me, does not affirm the identity of a young person as a pluralistic learner.

CJ: My kids were in the UK. We're in Norway at the moment. We've been living here for a year, [and are] going back in a couple of months. They've been in the Norwegian school out here and they've loved it. And so we were talking to our two eldest mainly about it and we were like: 'Why do you like it?' And they said: 'Well, you know, there is some maths and science. We sort of think that's OK, but there's loads of like design and there's loads of things where we get to draw and build things and we're outside a lot.' And, for them, they thought it was the best thing ever and they were still engaged in the classic disciplines but, you know, they felt overall they were enjoying the educational experience more. I mean my kids always liked school anyway. They were all pretty happy in the UK system, but they are just like 'Oh my God there is this like incredible other thing I can do.' I think that is amazing to see them enjoying that so much. Norway is a completely different economy, population system, it's a different thing. So, we can't just 'make it like Norway' which people say in the UK, which always winds me up.

But having seen that, it's interesting when we look at how constrained the UK system is and how that relates to funding and how that relates to autonomy of the school to make decisions independent of a political agenda, like Michael Gove's, 'we need to teach people Latin', being the extreme example of that. But when you have that freedom to engage with students on an individual level, and I know that there are a couple of schools that do this in London where they [students] can do this kind of enquiry-based learning where they [students] sort of basically define what they want to learn themselves. They say, 'I want to learn about why there's a river or how the canal works behind my house.' And then they go away and learn about the volume of water in the locks. They go away and learn about the stresses. There's this incredible empowerment around your learning where you're not being programmed.

There's this trade-off between [how] computer programmes work. You have to programme them but then there needs to be feedback from the operation, and that's kind of rather than just programming people as computers, making them part of the machinery as well.

MIB: Given all that you've experienced – work, life, being married to an educator – where do you feel the greatest inequalities lie within our education system?

CJ: I think the greatest inequality lies in the education system's current failing to identify how individual people are. By that I mean what their kind of life experience is to date, to that point and what their future aspirations are. It's basically not bespoke enough. It's not bespoke enough and I think, part of that is that it fails to recognize, it fails to redefine what success is. And I keep saying this to academics. They're allowing other people to define what success it and you'll never achieve somebody else's definition of success often, because success in academia is based around a monoculture. That's the problem. So, if you're not in that monoculture you're not going to get to that level of success but you can have that level of success which is no lower than that but is richer than that, than just writing papers and earning money. The education system's failure is also not recognizing how variable we all are and what has shaped us up to that point is.

Notes

1 Nazia Parveen, 2021, 'Children who organised Pimlico academy protest could be expelled', *The Guardian*, 16 April, www.theguardian.com/education/2021/apr/16/children-who-organised-pimlico-academy-protest-could-be-expelled, accessed 01.03.2022.

Period 6: Geography

Harvesting Potential

Again he began to teach beside the lake. Such a very large crowd gathered around him that he got into a boat on the lake and sat there, while the whole crowd was beside the lake on the land. He began to teach them many things in parables, and in his teaching he said to them: 'Listen! A sower went out to sow. And as he sowed, some seed fell on the path, and the birds came and ate it up. Other seed fell on rocky ground, where it did not have much soil, and it sprang up quickly, since it had no depth of soil. And when the sun rose, it was scorched; and since it had no root, it withered away. Other seed fell among thorns, and the thorns grew up and choked it, and it yielded no grain. Other seed fell into good soil and brought forth grain, growing up and increasing and yielding thirty and sixty and a hundredfold.' And he said, 'Let anyone with ears to hear listen!'
(Mark 4.1–9)

To teach beside the sea is to recognize that it is possible, because there is an understanding of the water, its nature and behaviour in different seasons, and whether it would accommodate this visiting crowd on its shores. The parable told is located in creation: beside the sea, on land, with the seeds and soil, in the presence of the sun and birds, before the thorns and finally with the grain. This is a story about us, but it is also a story about the world in which we live, how we interact with it, how we honour it, how it honours us, and how our lives are intertwined with air and earth. Who we are in the story, which kind of seeds, does not overcome the fact that, at some point, we all had the opportunity to fly through the air. All seeds flew from the hands of the creator to meet earth at a place of potential.

We pour our story into both sea and land. They bear witness to our presence. We bear witness to their telling of what we did and what we did not do, what we could have done and what we failed to do. Creation receives our story and reflects it back to us, because we are not set apart. The hospitality of the land and sea enables us to listen and live. To be guests on earth and temporary guardians means that we leave what is better for those to come; we build the story on which others will plant their own. We offer shelter from the harshness of the sun, we monitor the birds for the protection of the seeds, we uproot the thorns.

In the story we recognize that the seed must land. Every seed must land. There is no option on our planet for them to be suspended in the air, permanently in mid-flight. The kind of ground that meets the seed is not of the creator, but of us. We are called into the co-creative process of making the ground right, of responding to that call to protect, nurture and care for the seeds. The invitation brings much responsibility to align our actions to match the potential of each seed in order to reach full flourishing, and to enable others.

**

I can't remember how many trips off-site we had during my secondary school years. School trips, it feels to me, were rare. But I do remember Barcelona. A trip my family had scrimped to make possible in Year 9. Our Spanish teacher had the inspirational idea of inviting younger students to go on this trip with older ones who were already doing their GCSEs. This made for new friendships, 'sophisticated conversation' and no small amount of hilarity. Teenage girls from Brent visiting La Rambla, confidently employing their still-developing Spanish skills in situ, many of us, for the first time; the double-decker trains, the visit to a local school to meet our counterparts and, of course, the beach. For me, it was the beginning of a journey of the imagination, to new geographies and to begin to see what was possible, and how cultural understanding could be formed. In essence, it was transformative, and cemented my love of international travel and thirst for learning, about self and others, which has stayed with me ever since.

School trips

The challenge of the modern education system is that opportunities like the one just described may be few and far between, not least because of the resourcing needed to ensure that school trips are safe, purposeful and dare we say, fun. The Health and Safety Executive notes that:

> Misunderstandings about the application of health and safety law may, in some cases, discourage schools and teachers from organising such trips. These misunderstandings stem from a wide range of issues but may include frustrations about paperwork, fears of prosecution if the trip goes wrong, and the belief that a teacher will be sued if a child is injured.[1]

The reality, too, may be that, for some schools, the pressures of meeting attainment targets, preparing for internal and external assessments, as well as Ofsted inspections and meeting the tight schedules of the Schemes of Work may mean that trips are simply not possible. The right number of trained and/or knowledgeable staff may not be available to run the trips. There may not be enough space given in the school timetable to allow for these forms of experiential learning, despite the best intentions of teachers and senior leadership. If all these things were possible, and a school is able to run a trip locally, regionally, nationally or internationally, some school children may simply not be able to afford to go, therefore limiting this beneficial learning opportunity to those who could afford it.

It would be useful to have a national audit of off-site trips and visits, and compare these to the social economic situation of the schools through proxy measures such as Free School Meals or the Indices of Multiple Deprivation. This would give a clearer indication of how many school trips are offered to children at different schools, who has access to school trips, who actually goes on school trips and how many school trips a child has the opportunity to experience during their years in secondary school. For example, for those children who do not live near the sea, how many of them have seen such an expanse of water? How many have seen real livestock or have been to a gallery, museum, theatre show or concert? How close have the children been to the foot of a hill or mountain and what is their relationship to different spaces and places beyond the communities in which they live? It cannot be that school trips are only available to schools and learners who can afford it, because this only serves to deepen the inequalities evident in society and translated into our education system.

Schools – bricks and mortar

I wonder if, when you think back to your schooldays, you would describe your school as beautiful, or indeed any part of the buildings and outdoor spaces as beautiful? In my case, we had a beautiful path lined with what seemed to be giant plane trees that connected the main building and playground to the other parts of the school site. My secondary school was established in the late 1800s and so the red brick building became iconic for us. Its stairways, corridors and classrooms helped to define who we were (different year groups used different parts of the school) and contributed to a narrative about who we could be. Bells and resisting the temptation to run between classes to avoid being late framed our days. The playground and sports hall sharpened our sense of self, our leadership potential and the fierce competition that began in the classroom of the 'top sets' and spilled into most other areas of school life.

PERIOD 6: GEOGRAPHY

School buildings and spaces are not neutral. They say something about us as a society, what we value, and the messages we wish to convey about what school stands for and means.

> Schools are but one of many specialised adult-constructed and controlled institutions that place children in contained zones and structure their space and time ... However, children do not passively accept adult regulation nor adult attempts to shape their knowledge, identities or behaviour. Rather, children are competent social actors who employ a variety of strategies to contest, challenge or transgress adult spatial hegemony and boundaries ... both in schools ... and elsewhere ...[2]

For John Barker, Pam Alldred and others, schools can be analysed to see how they reinforce notions of power, 'crime and punishment', and status, and how they affirm or negate agency. They examine school-based internal exclusions and what the geography of these spaces can tell us about our relationship as a society with education.

Exclusion is now a permanent part of our education system:

> There are 2 types of exclusion: temporary (also known as 'fixed period exclusions') which can be for up to 45 school days, and permanent, which means a pupil can't return to the school they're excluded from.[3]

Government data presents a worrying picture of those who are temporarily excluded. We learn that 'White Gypsy and Roma pupils had the highest temporary exclusion rates in the 2018 to 2019 school year while pupils from the Chinese and Indian ethnic groups had the lowest temporary exclusion rates.'[4] From the ethnic groups used, we find the top percentages and number of students who face temporary exclusion:

- Gypsy Roma – 21.26% (5,813)
- Irish Traveller – 14.63% (925)
- Mixed White/Black Caribbean – 10.69% (13,337)
- Black Caribbean – 10.37% (9,112).[5]

The data suggests that, in terms of numbers, you are more likely to be temporarily excluded from school if you have Black heritage. Further, you find that:

> A fixed-term exclusion from school is a disciplinary measure that headteachers can use to deal with incidents of serious misbehaviour ... In order that exclusion does not function as a reward ('time off school'), and in order that excluded students receive education and adequate supervision, a growing number of schools in the UK (though rarely elsewhere) have developed school-based internal exclusion, also known as Seclusion Units or remove rooms (Department for Children, Schools and Families 2008).[6]

These temporary exclusions create new internal geographies within the school, with the sense that what is emphasized is separation and segregation within a punitive framework:

> The physical configuration of space is not simply neutral, but signifies much to the subjects who inhabit it ... The physical layout of Seclusion is clearly associated with punishment, mirroring the cells and partitioning found in prisons and other penal institutions ... Spatial arrangements and technologies produce a particular topography of power.[7]

If as a child or young person you are constantly disempowered, separated and isolated, what messages does this treatment reinforce and what reactions will this framework elicit? There is no sense that this is about flourishing but rather, perhaps, mirrors wider societal representations of 'crime and punishment' within a school setting. The geography remains imperialistic in tone and nature as children become subjects not active agents in the creation of meaningful solutions and enabling possibilities. Parents and carers are disempowered too, because often they have little choice in the matter if the school has stated what went wrong in terms of a child's behaviour and how this now needs to be 'fixed':

PERIOD 6: GEOGRAPHY

Therefore, the compulsive and penal nature of Seclusion is largely legitimised by parents and students as fair, appropriate and 'deserved' punishment – as one student put it, 'a good punishment for bad behaviour'. However, we need to recognise that simply because a dominant regime is powerful enough to reproduce itself as 'legitimate' in the eyes of those subject to its control, does not necessarily mean that it is indeed legitimate or, in this case, free from scrutiny in relation to the UK's adherence to the United Nations (1989) Convention on the Rights of the Child.[8]

The question therefore remains, how is all of this conducive to the child's flourishing? What does the geography of the school affirm and deny in and for our children? And is this the best we have to offer the next and each following generation? It may be worth reminding ourselves that children are not prisoners and teachers are not prison guards, and if that is the paradigm we are establishing and promoting, however implicitly, then the education system is broken.

Some argue that what is needed is a 'pedagogy of care' and 'ethics of care' in schools that humanize education:

> The aim of a pedagogy of care is to nurture young people's abilities to care and live together. Relatedness, responsiveness, meaning and connectedness are the undergirding concepts that sustain the theoretical construct of this paradigm ... Freire[9] proposed that the 'caring teacher' prefers a holistic education that fosters both academic and socio-emotional knowledge and understanding in students. In fact, socio-emotional knowledge is seen as a critical domain in education as it enables the building, maintaining and repairing of relationships that are central to human life. In the light of ethics of care, it is possible to examine how caring student-teacher relationships facilitate a renewed meaning to secondary school experience based on a humanistic approach.[10]

There is something at the centre of human geography that speaks to relationship, not just the human obsession with identification and categorization. This is not just an academic discipline and subject to be learned, but a culture to be established and practised. The notion of 'care' is central to education. We all know teachers who give beyond what is expected, and above their role and contractual hours, not because anyone asks them to, but simply because *they care*. We all recognize the teachers and staff in a school who go the extra mile to ensure children are safe and well attended to in school and often, more importantly, at home, when there is no one there to see the children. This is because these adults care about the children they teach and take their role of 'in loco parentis' seriously. Thus, if we are to take the ethics of care even further in our education system, we will need to examine how we reward as well as discipline:

> Margrain and Macfarlane[11] have thus asserted that ethics of care must also involve transforming school discipline protocols. This is necessary because the traditional view of discipline typically resolves conflicts through punishments and exclusion, whereas the perspective of care ethics seeks to resolve the causes that originated negative behaviour and prioritise the reestablishment of truncated relationships. The key concept derived from such an approach is restorative practice.[12]

Geography and the National Curriculum

The Geography National Curriculum (GNC) has gone through several iterations since its initial appearance in 1991, in 1995, 1999, 2008 and 2014:

> In the English school system, the term 'curriculum' has generally been used to describe the overall framework for what should be taught in state schools. Levels of prescription have

varied over time from the highly prescriptive original 1991 version with its 183 statements across five attainment targets, through to the 2008 curriculum which was contained in only four pages. It was only with the 1999 version that the curriculum was first given a specific set of aims and purposes ... Indeed, it could be argued that the latest (2014) version is not a curriculum in the true sense of the word, but merely an itemization of content that needs to be incorporated within any geography curriculum that is developed by a school.[13]

As with other subjects, successive governments have wanted to leave their mark and this can be seen in the 'iterations under Conservative (1991–7), Labour (1997–2010) and Coalition (2010–15) governments' in which 'the key drivers that have resulted in certain elements of curriculum content being introduced/removed, highlighted/marginalized' can be clearly identified and 'how the version of geography proposed by government could not be seen as neutral'.[14] The constant meddling of government in secondary school subjects means that there are regular shifts in both structure and content of what is being taught in schools, leaving teachers needing to make time to adapt to whatever changes are demanded by the Department of Education at a particular time.

Charles Rawding also writes that, in 1997, there was a 'shift in political direction heralded by the election of a New Labour Government' that 'led to education policies which explicitly linked educational improvement directly with economic growth, emphasizing skills for employment in order to create a highly skilled workforce'. It is here that we see a move away from the earlier versions of the curriculum:

> Unlike the 1991 and 1995 versions of the GNC, the 1999 version explicitly referenced learning across the curriculum with detailed listings in relation to the promotion of pupils' spiritual, moral, social and cultural development through geography, alongside the promotion of citizenship and key skills through geography.[15]

With the 2008 version there is yet another shift as the 'National Curriculum (2008–13) had a much stronger cross-curricular element to it, with the ten subjects famously diminished to a single line in the "Big Picture" diagram (Big Picture 2008) which was intended to summarize the whole curriculum'.[16] This, however, disappeared with the Coalition Government in 2010. The 2008 GNC also brought in notions of place which

> were heavily influenced by developments in cultural geography ... This way of thinking about place (as opposed to places) reflects postmodern approaches to the topic and is a very long way removed from the notions of place contained within the 1991 and 1995 versions of the GNC.[17]

While this development could have been seen to be an advancement, as the 'subject-specific innovations of the 2008 curriculum were focused almost entirely in human geography ... many aspects of physical geography appeared to be marginalized'.[18] By 2014, we find 'there has been an explicit (re)articulation of a physical–human binary to the subject – with the introductory Purpose of study requiring pupils to acquire 'a deep understanding of the Earth's key physical and human processes'.[19]

Geography as a subject in schools

There is something in all of these revisions of the Geography National Curriculum that may suggest a reductive instead of expansive view of the subject and its potential. It is important to remember that:

> The National Curriculum is essentially a minimal provision or entitlement. It does not have to be taught in private schools, but its similarity to earlier academic curriculums hints at its social control function and suggest that it is not suitable for advancing a liberal interpretation of the 1988 Education

Reform Act's curriculum objectives: that education should promote the spiritual, moral, cultural, mental and physical development of pupils at school and of society.[20]

Thus, we have a subject that has been manipulated and moulded according to political flavours and agenda. Though established as a compulsory subject within the National Curriculum, its content varies across schools and the provision within and beyond the classroom to experience the subject may be totally unequal. Geography was born out of a social necessity, and some would argue that its historical roots are still evident in the subject today:

> Our society's need for a school subject which would foster nationalism, imperialism and a positive view of the world of work, while teaching useful knowledge and skills to future clerks, merchants and soldiers, largely explains the entry of Geography into the school curriculum in the late nineteenth century and its subsequent revival and growth in the universities to meet the demand for qualified teachers ... Old geography textbooks reflect the racism, ethnocentrism, sexism and paternalism which pervades the early teaching of the subject.[21]

Some of these textbook challenges have been addressed in recent decades. Yet there is something greater that geography as a subject could address if reimagined with plural communities at a local, national and international levels in mind:

> School Geography has the potential to develop young people's understanding of their 'place' in the world and so help to form their identity. It can enable them to perceive the structures and processes which help and hinder their development, and can also foster the commitment to social justice and democracy, and the conserving, participatory and critical forms of citizenship, whereby they can seek to conserve or change those structures and processes and thereby help to create a better

world. The International Charter on Geographical Education[22] provides a comprehensive statement of such ideals and they are reflected in the aims, for Geography in the National Curriculum for England and Wales.[23]

Yet, the prescriptive nature of the curriculum and what teachers can and cannot teach, and when, underlines the difficulty in meeting this potential and speaking to how the subject can engender and promote a sense of active agency in learners. As John Huckle indicates '...in general it is becoming harder for geography teachers to work in ways which reflect progressive and radical ideals'.[24] Huckle posits the idea that 'school Geography is socially constructed and continues to play a role in the economic and cultural reproduction of our advanced capitalist society',[25] and that it could be so much more than this. In reading his work, I make the link between geography and citizenship, active engagement in society and the fostering of participatory democracy.

Writing at the beginning of the new millennium, Huckle pulls no punches about the failings of the way geography is presented and his sense of frustration is palpable:

> While school Geography's legacy of stereotyping has been exposed there has been less attention to the changing ideologies, or ideas which contribute to social regulation, which have pervaded the Geography curriculum. Existing studies[26] suggest that changing ideological emphases have left generations of pupils largely impotent as agents of social change. Nationalistic and imperialistic ideology taught them an unquestioning respect for nation and empire. Environmental determinism and natural regions taught them to accept a society shaped and limited by nature, which economic determinism taught them to accept the social relations of capitalism as normal and inevitable. The separation of the physical and human geography taught them a false separation of nature and society, while the subject's view of progress reinforced the modern faith in science, technology and bureaucracy.

PERIOD 6: GEOGRAPHY

Too much school Geography continues to draw solely on empiricist and positivist philosophies and so describes rather than explains the world. It fails to recognise power, conflict and agency, or to consider social alternatives, and can be seen to suggest to pupils that there are no real alternatives other than to accept the world largely as it is. Anyone doubting this assertion might try asking students who have recently passed A level Geography, what they understand by capitalism, green politics, or the state.[27]

Time has moved on, and we have to question whether Huckle's assertions still hold true. My hope is that there has been some movement in the subject, a re-energized approach that takes advantage of new theories in research and pedagogy to unlock the potential within the subject to 'help young people find their identity and place in the world – to find out how, why, with what, and where they belong, and to develop their sense of longing and belonging within a range of communities or collectives'.[28] Huckle's presentation of the questions that new curricula should aim to incorporate speaks to this wider ambition for the subject and to its undeniable potential to radically shift engagement and purpose in the minds and hearts of learners.

Reimagining geography

Huckle writes prophetically in 2002:

> Young people increasingly form their identities from the raw material of media and consumer culture and adopt a post-modern attitude which is sceptical of all authority, revels in artificiality, accepts a fragmented and placeless existence, regards security and identity as purely transitory, and welcomes an aestheticization of everyday life in which politics becomes the politics of style, presentation and gesture. Post-modernism threatens fragmentation, relativism and the

erosion of community, but it also offers the possibility of using new cultural technologies, products and attitudes to redefine identity, community and pleasure, as a means towards radical democracy. School Geography should acknowledge that young people face a world with few secure signposts yet display much commitment and imagination in using popular culture to construct meanings and identities. Our lessons should educate their sensibilities and interests by exploring how texts of all kinds represent places and environments and shape the geographical imagination, how the meaning of texts can be constructed and reconstructed to serve different interests, and how different senses of longing and belonging are produced in different places, among different groups, at different times.[29]

It may be that these words ring true and can be applied to the life and experiences of young people today. If we are to reimagine geography as a subject in schools, we will need to liberate it from the constraints of its history and realign with a new purpose that unites physical and human geography with the geosocial and geopolitical realities of the twenty-first century. Being able to offer a broader and deeper geographical imagination means linking the subject to others and examining landscapes, and peoples, communities and structures not only through an anthropocentric lens. We will need to develop a deeper understanding of human agency and responsibility, and our interdependence within the natural world. Geography can nurture our understanding of our connectedness across nation states, cultures, beliefs and physical spaces. Place becomes a call towards a coherent understanding of what it means to be human as opposed to a divisive element to demarcate belonging.

Sustainable travel will need to be at the core of learning to foster experiential learning beyond the classroom. This will need to be protected to enable equal access to opportunities and experiences. Societal inequalities can be further exposed through the study of geography, with students encouraged to realize their potential to change the status quo. We do not have to accept the world as it currently is, and we can encourage current and future learners to imagine the world as it could be. This begins with a new approach to school sites and buildings, using local talent and craftspeople to construct physical spaces that are created for and by the community. Beauty can be inspiring, and our schools need to be beautiful as well as celebratory of learning and humanity. Our schools cannot continue to resemble prisons with long corridors, square classrooms and rows of desks and chairs as if these are the bedrock of flourishing. We know that they are not.

Geography as a subject need not be reductive, but should raise the expectation of active citizenship and meet it with the tools to read and understand communities and societies so that the collaborative and co-creative process of democracy can be lived, and felt, and protected. In and through this subject we can reimagine active agency rooted in the tangibility of the physical earth, of real people, in which we are all held accountable because we can see, and hear and feel our interconnectedness and respond equitably to this reality, that is neither virtual nor artificial, but anchored in our bodies, living organisms planted in nature.

Notes

1 Health and Safety Executive, 2011, 'School trips and outdoor learning activities Tackling the health and safety myths', *Health and Safety Executive*, www.hse.gov.uk/services/education/school-trips.pdf, accessed 01.03.2022.
2 John Barker, Pam Alldred, Mike Watts et al., 2010, 'Pupils or prisoners? Institutional geographies and internal exclusion in UK secondary schools', *AREA*, 42(3), pp. 378–86, p. 379.
3 UK Government, 24 February 2021, *Temporary Exclusions*. www.ethnicity-facts-figures.service.gov.uk/education-skills-and-training/absence-and-exclusions/pupil-exclusions/latest, accessed 06.04.2022.
4 UK Government, 24 February 2021, *Temporary Exclusions*.
5 UK Government, 24 February 2021, *Temporary Exclusions*.
6 Barker, Alldred, Watts et al. 'Pupils or prisoners?', p. 379.
7 Barker, Alldred, Watts et al. 'Pupils or prisoners?', p. 382.

8 Barker, Alldred, Watts et al. 'Pupils or prisoners?', p. 382.

9 Paulo Freire, 1998, *Pedagogy of freedom: Ethics, democracy, and civic courage*, Lanham, MD: Rowman & Littlefield Publishers.

10 Letitia Hochstrasser Fickel, Maria Nieto Angel, Sonja MacFarlane et al., 2017, 'Humanising Secondary School Contexts: Learning from Aotearoa New Zealand and Peru', *Knowledge Cultures* 5(6), p. 49.

11 Valerie Margrain and Angus H. Macfarlane, 2011, *Responsive pedagogy: Engaging restoratively with challenging behaviour*, Wellington, New Zealand: NZCER Press.

12 Fickel, Nieto Angel, MacFarlane et al., 'Humanising Secondary School Contexts', p. 49.

13 Charles Rawding, 2015, 'Constructing the Geography Curriculum' in Graham Butt (ed.), *MasterClass in Geography Education: Transforming Teaching and Learning*, London: Bloomsbury Academic, pp. 67–80, p. 69.

14 Rawding, 'Constructing the Geography Curriculum', p. 70.

15 Rawding, 'Constructing the Geography Curriculum', p. 71.

16 Rawding, 'Constructing the Geography Curriculum', p. 73.

17 Rawding, 'Constructing the Geography Curriculum', p. 73.

18 Rawding, 'Constructing the Geography Curriculum', p. 73.

19 Rawding, 'Constructing the Geography Curriculum', p. 74.

20 John Huckle, 2002, 'Towards a critical school Geography' in *Teaching Geography in Schools: A Reader*, London: Routledge, pp. 255–65, p. 257.

21 Huckle, 'Towards a critical school Geography', p. 256.

22 The International Charter on Geographical Education, 1992, available from www.igu-cge.org/1992-charter/, accessed 01.03.2022.

23 Huckle, 'Towards a critical school Geography', p. 255.

24 Huckle, 'Towards a critical school Geography', p. 255.

25 Huckle, 'Towards a critical school Geography', p. 256.

26 Rob Gilbert, 1984, *The Impotent Image: Reflections of Ideology in the Secondary Curriculum*, Lewes: Falmer Press.

27 Huckle, 'Towards a critical school Geography', pp. 256–7.

28 Huckle, 'Towards a critical school Geography', p. 261.

29 Huckle, 'Towards a critical school Geography', p. 262.

Period 7: Lunch

Eating is a Right not a Privilege

> Now when Jesus heard this, he withdrew from there in a boat to a deserted place by himself. But when the crowds heard it, they followed him on foot from the towns. When he went ashore, he saw a great crowd; and he had compassion for them and cured their sick. When it was evening, the disciples came to him and said, 'This is a deserted place, and the hour is now late; send the crowds away so that they may go into the villages and buy food for themselves.' Jesus said to them, 'They need not go away; you give them something to eat.' They replied, 'We have nothing here but five loaves and two fish.' And he said, 'Bring them here to me.' Then he ordered the crowds to sit down on the grass. Taking the five loaves and the two fish, he looked up to heaven, and blessed and broke the loaves, and gave them to the disciples, and the disciples gave them to the crowds. And all ate and were filled; and they took up what was left over of the broken pieces, twelve baskets full. And those who ate were about five thousand men, besides women and children.
> (Matthew 14.13–21)

If you had walked a long way or had been so engrossed in work and learning for most of the day, you would expect a good and filling meal, not because you had needed to walk or work to deserve it but because it was your human right. The crowds in this story may have heard their stomachs rumbling and experienced the loss of energy from the day's heat and begun to expect. Jesus recognized their expectation probably before his disciples came to him to tell him their logical assessment of the situation. The remoteness and lack of access to local amenities mean that there really is no other option but to send the people away.

In the absence of external resourcing, there is provision from within. There is a review of what is available and what is possible. Jesus looks to the people for what they already have and how this can be transformed for the many. In John's account it is a boy who provides the five loaves and two fishes. The child remains in the story, and we see that providing for the children first matters. All can eat and all will be filled if we are to find a source that can be multiplied for the good of the many.

There is also something about the abundance of relief that speaks to a greater capacity that, as humans, we may need to dig deep to provide. People would have had seconds and thirds, not out of greed but so that they could be filled. There is also the clarity of place. The crowds were able 'to sit down on the grass' to eat their meal. There was space for that rest and repose. We hope that there was some relative sense of comfort, despite the fact that the 'hour is now late'. Could it have been dark? If so, some form of light would have been needed and people would have needed to gather in as the temperature dropped. The feeding was the first of many needs to be met, and the most essential.

The crowd were satisfied and would probably have been able to have made their return journey home. There seems to have been enough to take with them, in the leftovers available after the meal. Feeding gives capacity for other things, and this needs to be recognized. It is the beginning of provision, not the end. In the journey to and from Jesus we receive more than we can ever give, and this is a mark of the divine. We cannot replicate or replace; we can only reflect divine love so that others are drawn into its nourishment.

***

The memories I have around food and secondary school all centre around one word: sugar. I remember the discussions in

PERIOD 7: LUNCH

the playground over which chocolate bar was supreme and to which chocolate bar we were pledging our allegiance. I was most definitely in the Boost corner. Perfect in every way. I remember the corner shop right outside the school where we would congregate to buy ice lollies after school, laughing as they made our tongues pink, blue or orange. I remember the other shop, nearer home, with Mr and Mrs Fernandes waving as I popped in to say hello on the way to school. That was the shop of knowledge, where I got my magazines and newspapers and the place where I was known.

My mother reminds me that I used to get £5 per day for the bus fare (when I didn't walk) to and from school and lunch. This was the nineties so £5 went a long way. We were not allowed off-site, so we had to make do with whatever was supplied. Thankfully, my allergies had not yet been diagnosed, so I ate pretty much anything in my teenage years, though I left meat behind after dabbling for a bit following a vegetarian upbringing. I do remember the canteen being too small and the overcrowding and being rushed in and out so another class could have their lunch.

What saved me when I moved from my secondary school in north-west London to my sixth form in south-west London was the Education Maintenance Allowance (EMA), piloted in 1999, ideal for my last year and a half of schooling. The scheme gave payments to students aged 16–19 from low-income families who were attending full-time courses in schools and colleges.[1] This meant that I got £30 per week, which paid for my travel and some lunch on the days I was at sixth form college. We were allowed off site to buy lunch at 17, so I could start to experiment with delis and more sophisticated lunches because I was older and, well, more sophisticated. I also had my second part-time job working at Mothercare in Brent Cross, so I was earning a wage to supplement my studies. Now I look back I think I spent a lot of my monthly salary at Grant and Cutler, the foreign language book shop on Great Marlborough Street. Travelling into central London to lose myself in its tightly packed shelves was just joyful. Without the EMA I am not sure how I would have managed to get materials for sixth form college, pay for travel and lunch.

The issue of school meals, who provides them, what is provided, who should have access to them and how they should be administered, has been a topic of great interest over the past two decades. In 2005, UK chef, Jamie Oliver fronted a television series, 'Jamie's School Dinners' which, in four episodes, explored what our children were eating in schools. In the show, he revealed how little was spent on pupils' meals at some schools. This led to the 'Feed Me Better' campaign, which attracted 271,677 signatures of support for Oliver's petition to improve the state of school meals, and which was duly handed over to Downing Street in the following year.[2] The government at the time pledged to spend a further £280 million on school meals. The introduction of school meal standards in 2006,[3] aimed to offer diverse, good quality and healthy provision of food in schools.

The new school meal standards were met with alarm from some quarters, with some decrying the impact on the provider of meals in schools. One article detailed the following:

> The head of one of the UK's largest school dinner caterers has rubbished claims that stricter food rules will bring about the collapse of the secondary school meals system.
>
> Some caterers have raised fears that new nutrient-based standards, due to launch in secondary schools in England this September, will exacerbate the ongoing decline in the secondary school meals market – which saw uptake fall to a new low of 37.2% last year – threatening the commercial future of the service. But Jane Bristow, managing director of Sodexo Education, which feeds children at 740 schools across the UK and Ireland, insisted that healthy school meals were both achievable and commercially viable.[4]

The comment from the caterer highlights a key issue in school meal provision: the food is only as good as the organization supplying it and the people cooking it. Inherent in our secondary education system is inequality of and in provision, when it comes to school meals, which is entirely dependent on the cost and stipulations of the contract signed with the caterer. It would be interesting to discover how many parents know who is providing their children's meals.

It would be a sobering exercise if parents and carers went into school for a week and had the same meals their children were eating. A catering company given the task of providing food parcels for children during the pandemic scrimped on food to maximize profits, with inadequate quality and quantity of food arriving in low-income homes. The government was forced to change its course of action, 'in response to images of pitiful food parcels shared by parents on social media. The uproar prompted an apology from the country's largest school catering provider, Chartwells, and a move by industry body LACA to update its guidance on what hampers should contain.'[5]

It is a testimony to how we see children that our catering contracts in schools are given to the same companies that run prisons. Some caterers do not provide value for money, meaning that elements of a meal (for example, drinks) are not covered by the free school meal allocation. Some children in effect have to top up their free school meals to ensure that they are well fed and have all the different nutritional elements that they need. Private contractors involved in the delivery of school meals for our children need to be scrutinized because their priorities may differ to those of parents, carers and teachers.

From the introduction of food standards in schools in 2006, school meals have remained in the public's sightline as some things have changed, but much has stayed the same. It is important to remember that, in the summer of 2012 the government announced that it would take further action:

> The government has today announced that it has asked the co-founders of LEON restaurant chain, Henry Dimbleby and John Vincent, to examine school food across the country. They will create an action plan to accelerate improvement in

school food and determine the role of food more broadly in school life.

Over the last decade there has been a big change of attitude towards school food and significant improvement in many schools. This is the result of work done by a large array of people, including the School Food Trust, associated charities such as School Food Matters, and Jamie Oliver's Foundation – not to mention the individual cooks, teachers, parents, pupils, outside caterers and local authorities who have embraced the cause.

However, in both maintained schools and academies there is a lot of work still to do. School Food Trust research shows that:

- take-up of school lunches is just 38% in secondary schools and 44% in primary schools;
- only 22.5% of schools provide at least one portion of fruit and veg per pupil every day;
- half of secondary schools offer pizzas and starchy food cooked in oil on most days;
- a third of young people are not choosing a healthy balanced meal at school.[6]

Between 2006 and 2020, there has been a growing coalition of support for improving the quality of school meals and ensuring that children are well provided for in terms of both nutritional value and healthy eating. Organizations such as Chefs in Schools[7] and School Food Matters[8] have ensured that schools meals remain on the policy agenda.

Free school meals

The government guidance on eligibility for free school meals states:

Free school meals (FSM) are available to pupils in receipt of, or whose parents are in receipt of, one or more of the following benefits:

- Universal Credit (provided you have an annual net earned income of no more than £7,400, as assessed by earnings from up to three of your most recent assessment periods)
- Income Support
- Income-based Jobseeker's Allowance
- Income-related Employment and Support Allowance
- Support under Part VI of the Immigration and Asylum Act 1999
- The guarantee element of Pension Credit
- Child Tax Credit (provided you're not also entitled to Working Tax Credit and have an annual gross income of no more than £16,190)
- Working Tax Credit paid for four weeks after you stop qualifying for Working Tax Credit.[9]

Free school meals mean the difference between a child eating well and going hungry. The provision of FSM aids families who are struggling and reliant on external support for feeding their children. There should be no reason why, today, we cannot feed our children in England and within the UK. It is important to remember, however, that free school meals do not feed every child in a low-income family in England. The Child Poverty Action Group highlights that:

> Prior to the pandemic, at least two in five school-age children – 1.3 million – who lived below the UK's poverty line were not entitled to free school meals, new analysis from Child Poverty Action Group (CPAG) shows. All of these children are in families in low paid work but do not qualify because of stringent eligibility criteria, the analysis finds.
> CPAG estimates that another 100,000 school children across the UK (who are not covered by universal infant free school meals) are in families with no recourse to public funds

because of their immigration status. Many of these children will be living well below the poverty line but are not usually eligible for means-tested free school meals.[10]

As a result of the pandemic revealing and exacerbating the structural inequalities that were already present in our society, the subject of free school meals is now in the public consciousness as never before. Food poverty and insecurity existed before Covid-19 and will still exist when we move from coronavirus being a pandemic to a permanent presence:

> The proportion of children eligible varies considerably across the country, but generally matches recognised trends surrounding regional deprivation and wealth. For example, almost a quarter of pupils in the north-east of England are eligible compared with about 13% of pupils in the south-east.[11]

In 2020, Manchester United footballer, Marcus Rashford, campaigned around FSM. He focused on the gap in provision between the academic year and the school holidays, with families having to fend for themselves to ensure that their children were fed. The government, having initially stated that there would be no extension of FSM in the school holidays, had to make an embarrassing U-turn under the interrogating gaze of an unimpressed general public. FSM were to be provided through vouchers for eligible children. It was the replacement of these vouchers by food parcels which led to another government U-turn.

Rashford's campaign led to the establishment of the #End ChildFoodPoverty Task Force, bringing together a coalition of businesses and charities to campaign for three key changes: 1) to extend the Holiday Activity and Food Programme to all areas in England, to all children in receipt of Free School Meals; 2) to increase the value of Healthy Start vouchers to £4.25. These are vouchers which support pregnant women or those with children under the age of 4; 3) to expand FSM to all under-16s where a parent or carer is in receipt of Universal Credit or equivalent benefit.[12] The first two have been achieved. The government has yet to move on the third.

The campaign to provide FSM for children during the school holidays underlines the level of food insecurity many families face. The groundswell of support for Marcus Rashford's campaign hit a nerve. The realization that eating was a right, not a privilege framed the responses to the campaign, with local businesses and councils[13] defying the government to support the feeding of children outside the academic year. This was an issue about which the public really cared. There was a sense that parts of society were beginning to see the feeding of children as a collective responsibility.

The Food Foundation's report on how the Covid-19 pandemic has affected access to food across UK households is a difficult but essential read. The report underlines groups with higher levels of food insecurity including households with children, those living with the extremely clinically vulnerable and minority ethnic groups.[14] Food insecurity is defined as 'limited or uncertain availability of nutritionally adequate and safe foods or limited or uncertain ability to acquire acceptable foods in socially acceptable ways'.[15] There is a clear sense in reading the report that the drivers of food insecurity (not enough money, isolation, lack of supply and other reasons) have been worsened by the pandemic.

In relation to FSM, the report makes the following recommendation:

> An urgent and comprehensive review into Free School Meal policy across the UK. To support all low-income children and families in the aftermath of the pandemic, the review should ensure Free School Meals are delivering maximum nutritional and educational impact and promoting children's learning and wellbeing throughout the school day. It should review the current eligibility threshold to make sure no disadvantaged children are missing out on the benefits of a Free School Meal.[16]

There is the recognition that things were not fine before the pandemic and are certainly not fine now. We cannot go back to the way things were, as writer Rebecca Solnit reminds us (chapter 1). We have to reimagine a better future and better provision for our children and young people. We have to work harder to realign our priorities with their flourishing and work to establish a secure platform on which they can build future pathways.

It makes no sense to say that you care for children, but do not want to shift funds around to feed them. If governments can allocate £56 billion to HS2,[17] then surely feeding the nation's children is a small financial outlay in comparison? The truth of the matter is that the current government does not care enough about low-income families and those struggling to survive the added financial impact of the pandemic. To feed a child is symbolic of a greater investment than just that meal. It is about seeing that food is only one of the first needs that ought to be met, and taking into account the impact that food insecurity will have on each individual. There is an underlying attitude in the war of attrition on FSM that it is the fault of those without and that they 'need to work harder or do better' to get themselves out of the situation that they are in. What needs to be underlined instead is the fact that we are part of a deeply unequal society, and these inequalities grow deeper and broader in each year of inaction by government.

Reimagining school meals

The feeding of children is a moral imperative. We need to feed, protect and safeguard children from the desperation and despair of sleeping and waking up hungry. Hunger does not enable and affirm a child. Hunger does not lead to full flourishing. Hunger does not aid the potential of a child being fulfilled. There is no shrinking away from this reality. There is a clear indication from numerous reports that we need to review the FSM policy and that we also need to provide more for those who are receiving state help, recognizing the real economic increases in food costs.

School meals have become a political battleground for how we think about and measure poverty and the impact of poverty on children. No one could argue with the fact that not eating and not having a good meal affects children in many ways: their physical development, mental health and well-being, and cognition. So, what if school meals and lunchtime became less of an event in the day and more of a part of the day's learning journey? What if lunchtime was not squeezed in between lessons but was the end of the learning day after which students could deepen their knowledge of nature, their environment and the sources of the ingredients that had just eaten?

A new kind of lunchtime would develop 'health literacy', which according to the World Health Organisation has lasting impact:

> Improving health literacy in populations provides the foundation on which citizens are enabled to play an active role in improving their own health, engage successfully with community action for health, and push governments to meet their responsibilities in addressing health and health equity.[18]

In addition to the eating of a well-balanced, tasty and nutritious meal, and the opportunity to socialize with friends, lunchtime could develop into a learning programme around food. Initiatives such as the Hackney School of Food[19] are already heading in this direction. Children could develop their knowledge of food and their confidence in being able to make positive decisions about what they eat. This sort of programme could involve developing school and community kitchen gardens, reintroducing cooking classes, and speaking to local producers about their work and the journey from field to plate. Schools in cities could be supplied by local, urban growers, while more rural schools would form direct relationships with the farmers and growers local to them. Thus, the feeding of our children during and beyond the school day becomes a collective endeavour, resulting in the embedding of the school as a community enterprise. This kind of learning programme would necessitate a complete redesign of the school day, liberation from the curriculum and an ambitious building programme that enabled the addition of the necessary facilities to schools.

Notes

1 Mike Fletcher, 2000, *Education Maintenance Allowances: The Impact on Further Education*, FEDA, available from https://dera.ioe.ac.uk/4277/1/ADD_Education_maintenance_allowances_-_the_impact_on_further_education.pdf, accessed 01.03.2022.

2 BBC News, 2006, 'Oliver's school meal crusade goes on', 4 September, http://news.bbc.co.uk/1/hi/uk/5313882.stm, accessed 01.03.2022.

3 UK Government, 'School meals - healthy eating standards', *Gov.uk*, www.gov.uk/school-meals-healthy-eating-standards, accessed 01.03.2022.

4 Chris Druce, 2009, 'Sodexo says new rules can work in secondary schools', *Caterer & Hotelkeeper*, 198(4561), p. 4.

5 Freddie Whittaker, 2021, 'Food parcels fiasco: How the pandemic exposed free school meals failures ... again', *Schools Week*, 14 January, https://schoolsweek.co.uk/food-parcels-fiasco-how-the-pandemic-exposed-free-school-meals-failures-again/, accessed 01.03.2022.

6 Department for Education, 2012, 'Improving school food', 4 July, *Gov.uk*, www.gov.uk/government/news/improving-school-food, accessed 01.03.2022.

7 Chefs in Schools, www.chefsinschools.org.uk/.

8 School Food Matters, 'About Us', *School Food Matters*, www.schoolfoodmatters.org/about-us, accessed 01.03.2022.

9 Department for Education, 2018, *Free school meals Guidance for local authorities, maintained schools, academies and free schools*, April, https://assets.publishing.service.gov.uk/government/uploads/system/uploads/attachment_data/file/700139/Free_school_meals_guidance_Apr18.pdf, p. 5.

10 Child Poverty Action Group, 2020, 'Two in Five UK Children Under the Poverty Line are Not Eligible for Free School Meals', 3 December, *Child Poverty Action Group*, https://cpag.org.uk/news-blogs/news-listings/two-five-uk-children-under-poverty-line-are-not-eligible-free-school-meals, accessed 01.03.2022.

PERIOD 7: LUNCH

11 BBC News, 2020, 'Free school meals: How many children can claim them', *BBC News*, 26 October, www.bbc.co.uk/news/54693906/, accessed 01.03.2022.

12 #EndChildFoodPoverty, https://endchildfoodpoverty.org/

13 Patrick Butler, Richard Adams and Peter Walker, 2020, 'Councils back Rashford and pledge to provide school meals over holidays', *The Guardian*, 23 October, www.theguardian.com/society/2020/oct/23/councils-across-england-pledge-to-provide-free-school-meals-over-holidays, accessed 01.03.2022.

14 The Food Foundation, *A Crisis within a Crisis: The Impact of Covid-19 on Household Food Security: Insights from Food Foundation Surveys on how the Pandemic has Affected Food Access in the UK (March 2020 to January 2021)*, available from https://foodfoundation.org.uk/wp-content/uploads/2021/03/FF_Impact-of-Covid_FINAL.pdf, accessed 01.03.2022.

15 The Food Foundation, *A Crisis within a Crisis*, p. 5.

16 The Food Foundation, *A Crisis within a Crisis*, p. 4.

17 Tom Herbert and Browen Weatherby, 2020, 'How much has been spent on the HS2 so far and what is the proposed train route?', *London Evening Standard*, 11 February, www.standard.co.uk/news/uk/hs2-train-route-budget-spend-a4359426.html, accessed 01.03.2022.

18 World Health Organisation, www.who.int/activities/improving-health-literacy.

19 Hackney School of Food, www.hackneyschooloffood.com/.

Period 8: History

Whose History is it Anyway?

Then Jesus said, 'There was a man who had two sons. The younger of them said to his father, "Father, give me the share of the property that will belong to me." So he divided his property between them. A few days later the younger son gathered all he had and travelled to a distant country, and there he squandered his property in dissolute living. When he had spent everything, a severe famine took place throughout that country, and he began to be in need. So he went and hired himself out to one of the citizens of that country, who sent him to his fields to feed the pigs. He would gladly have filled himself with the pods that the pigs were eating; and no one gave him anything. But when he came to himself he said, "How many of my father's hired hands have bread enough and to spare, but here I am dying of hunger! I will get up and go to my father, and I will say to him, 'Father, I have sinned against heaven and before you; I am no longer worthy to be called your son; treat me like one of your hired hands.'" So he set off and went to his father. But while he was still far off, his father saw him and was filled with compassion; he ran and put his arms around him and kissed him. Then the son said to him, "Father, I have sinned against heaven and before you; I am no longer worthy to be called your son." But the father said to his slaves, "Quickly, bring out a robe – the best one – and put it on him; put a ring on his finger and sandals on his feet. And get the fatted calf and kill it, and let us eat and celebrate; for this son of mine was dead and is alive again; he was lost and is found!" And they began to celebrate.

'Now his elder son was in the field; and when he came and approached the house, he heard music and dancing. He called one of the slaves and asked what was going on. He

replied, "Your brother has come, and your father has killed the fatted calf, because he has got him back safe and sound." Then he became angry and refused to go in. His father came out and began to plead with him. But he answered his father, "Listen! For all these years I have been working like a slave for you, and I have never disobeyed your command; yet you have never given me even a young goat so that I might celebrate with my friends. But when this son of yours came back, who has devoured your property with prostitutes, you killed the fatted calf for him!" Then the father said to him, "Son, you are always with me, and all that is mine is yours. But we had to celebrate and rejoice, because this brother of yours was dead and has come to life; he was lost and has been found.'"
(Luke 15.11–32)

There is something unbelievably annoying about this story. It is the absence of the mother, and any sense that she had a role to play in the unfolding of this story. Presence and absence categorize the interplay between parent and son and the relationship between the two brothers. Presence: the urgent needs and wants of the younger son to get away and make his own life. Presence: the response of the father by granting his son's wishes and responding to his request. Presence: the delight of the father at his son's return. Absence: the lack of self-interrogation in addition to the questioning by the father. Absence: the mother of the two brothers. Absence: the delight of the older brother at his brother's return. In this story we see the history of the son written and presented in binary terms: younger son leaves home, son messes up, son returns and is forgiven, older brother is angry (and rightly so) and is left to wonder what kind of father he actually has. Yet we know that life is not binary nor clear-cut, and that opportunities, access and possibilities are not open to all.

Who writes and tells our history gives us or negates our identity. Who is posited as hero or villain, good or bad, right or wrong, can shape our lives and responses, not only to ourselves but to others. Flourishing is contingent not only on what is in the story, but who is allowed to tell that story, and who is missing and absent from it. Talent and academic, sporting and artistic potential can be visible, but opportunity nowhere to be seen. Opportunity can be present but access to that opportunity lacking. The unforgiving nature of the societies in which we live leaves its mark. There is often no time to reflect, or grieve, or mourn. The message that competition reigns supreme becomes like dye, changing the colour of every area of our lives. We are majestic in our sense of individuality and self-reliance, but our stories often only develop meaning and richness when we see how they intertwine with the stories of others.

We are never allowed personal failure or wrong decisions, because somehow these mean that we do not matter or that we are not as worthy as others. Yet, the fundamental truth is that there is a divine space of acceptance and readiness, a space in which love waits for us. The readiness is for us, no matter the permutations of life, to fulfil our full potential, to flourish, to thrive. The waiting is for us, to learn from the past, from our stories, his-stories, her-stories, and their-stories, and recognize that we are connected. Our living and dying is connected. Our very breath is connected to the surroundings in which we find ourselves. Our flourishing, or lack thereof, is also deeply connected.

***

One of my most memorable lessons in history did not happen in the classroom. It took place when our history teacher arranged for us to meet and listen to a survivor of the Holocaust. We were in one of the halls in school, seated and utterly captivated by this elderly man, whom we had never met, but who spoke with such dignity. What a privilege that was. As secondary school students we were encouraged to send our storyteller questions based on what we had heard. We sent so many questions that he came back for a second visit to the school, which

PERIOD 8: HISTORY

I was very sad to miss as I was not in school that day. His story of living under authoritarian rule, terror, tragedy and loss was framed by a sense of duty that we had to know and never deny, to remember and pass on what we had heard and learned. He was a living testimony to how history needed to be told over and over again, with different voices being heard in that retelling, voices that speak to the truth of what was lived and what had to be survived.

A history of the subject in schools

Let us be clear before we begin: history teaching and learning as we know it is never the full story. The history I studied at school may or may not have been different from the one that generations before and after studied, but what we probably have in common would be: Henry VIII and his six wives and World War Two and the defeat of the Nazis by allied forces. What is left out is just as important as what is included. Inequality intersects with history (the subject) in many ways, and the challenge of developing and embedding a curriculum that speaks to our shared histories as well as the significant community and global histories is still evident today. It is important, however, to remember that history must be inclusive and plural, lest it risks becoming fertile soil for some of those authoritarian eras in our human story to which we should never return. What we also should acknowledge is that:

> There is a need to ensure that any debate on history in schools accepts as a starting premise the complex mosaic of localities, nations and communities that make up the histories of the British-Irish Isles.[1]

This complexity is not guaranteed to be protected by any Department for Education as it wields its axe through school curricula, nor by any Secretary of State for Education. History always seems to be the battleground where any government plants its flag and stakes its reputation when it comes to education reform. Perhaps it is because governments know that whoever controls the narrative, controls how stories are told, retold and remembered.

The purpose for teaching history has often been linked to some form of moral teaching:

> For much of the time that history has been part of the school curriculum in England, perhaps the most important justification for its role has been to serve as a moral exemplar for young people. An early manifestation of this was Lord Palmerston's rationale for the opening of the National Portrait Gallery in London:
> *There cannot be a greater incentive to mental exertion, to good conduct on the part of the living, than for them to see before them the features of those who have done things which are worthy of our admiration and whose example we are induced to imitate.*[2]
>
> This justification for school history was reiterated by the Board of Education's Suggestions for the Consideration of History Teachers in 1905: *The lives of great men and women, carefully selected from all stations of life, will furnish the most impressive examples of obedience, loyalty, courage, strenuous effort, serviceableness, indeed, all the qualities which make for good citizenship.*[3]

I am not exactly sure what I, as a Black British woman can learn from Henry VIII in terms of qualities 'which make for good citizenship' but I do know that at school I never saw myself reflected in any of the lessons I had or any of the topics that were presented. This idea of the subject holding the power to transform the lives of those who engage with it is defeated by the often reductive and limiting exposition of the subject at school:

> As late as the 1980s, a former Chief HMI (Her Majesty's Inspector) for history parodied the form of school history

PERIOD 8: HISTORY

still prevailing in English schools as: Largely British, or rather Southern English: Celts looked in to starve, emigrate or rebel; the North, to invent looms or work in mills; abroad was of interest once it was part of the Empire; foreigners were either, sensibly, allies, or rightly, defeated. Skills – did we even use the word? – were mainly those of recalling accepted facts about famous dead Englishmen, and communicated in a very eccentric literary form, the examination length essay.[4]

That was then, but what about the 1990s and beyond? As other subjects:

> The history national curriculum was first introduced in 1990. Before that, schools had the freedom to teach history or not. Few went as far as deleting it entirely from the curriculum, but many merged it in with other subjects, or reduced the time available as more 'modern' subjects appeared on the timetable in the 1970s and 1980s. And there was no agreed syllabus – so children might encounter a mix of historical events and periods which did not connect up to give them an overview of past change and development.[5]

Clearly something had to change. The introduction of the National Curriculum (NC) ensured that history could be accessed by all children in all schools. The NC also aimed to bring some form of standardization and framework to teaching in different contexts and ages. Teachers would be able to fall back on a structure that could be populated by different themes and topics, but with a sense that connections could be made to show how communities, movements and nations developed. Another interesting consequence of developing a NC, of course, is that:

> It makes it economically worthwhile for publishers and broadcasters to produce materials to support the curriculum as they know what topics children will be studying at what age. The quality and range of printed, electronic and online

resources to support the teaching of history in schools today are superb.[6]

Think of all those documentaries on television and radio, as well as printed and online magazines that focus on history, and which shape their content and publication schedules around both national celebrations and what is being taught in schools.

Then came a new government and 'the accession to power of a Coalition Government dominated by the Conservative Party in May 2010 accelerated the momentum of forces calling for the return of the Victorian model of school history'.[7] In the following years, the Secretary of State, Michael Gove, would focus on secondary education reform that touched every subject, the effects of which are still being felt today. The new history curriculum would be hugely controversial:

> Michael Gove's draft history curriculum was published as part of the consultation process for the whole national curriculum on 7 February 2013. It prescribed a mainly English focus on British history with eight-to-eleven-year-olds expected to study from ancient times to 1714, and older students from 1714 to the premiership of Margaret Thatcher (1979–90). The draft became a site of some contention. Many events, including military encounters and victories, were listed as having to be learnt. It would attract conflicting responses from two sets of 'elite' networks which Michael Gove would be forced to attempt to reconcile through 'round table' meetings in the period from March to June 2013. These could be categorized as: (a) conservative-traditional with an enthusiasm for national history set in a consecutive chronological framework; and (b) liberal-inclusive with an enthusiasm for contextualizing national history both globally and in a more flexible chronological framework.[8]

The political agenda behind this new curriculum cannot be denied. It is clear that 'the Coalition took up a sophisticated stance in the presentation of its agenda of restoration, which links excellence and traditionalism to opportunity and social mobility ... what might also be called "policies of nostalgia".[9] Looking back to past glories affords the opportunity to forgive present crises and inequalities. The allure of the rose-tinted glass often masks the presence of those whose lived realities were less than rosy. It also perpetuates lies and binaries that do not reflect the complexities of history.

What was present or absent from the new curriculum also added more fuel to the debate around its launch:

> There were particular concerns around how the new curriculum acknowledged, or elided, issues of racial and ethnic diversity and the position of Black histories within this narrative. Our own critique[10] highlighted the ways in which the idea of 'Britain' itself excluded its more ethnically and socially diverse roots and routes, positioning migrants, Black and minority ethnic and religious communities at the margins of the nation rather than as an integral part of 'our Island story'.[11]

Gove's idea of 'island story' renders in the singular what has always been in the plural. To be an island is to have a historic identity as a place of movement, with stories of peoples coming and leaving this island, with their contributions, legacies and achievements. Notable key national and global Black figures were absent from the new history curriculum:

> The focus on British history in the revised curriculum was reduced to 'a minimum' of 40% at GCSE level and 20% at A-level. Under public pressure, such as the Operation Black Vote[12] campaign, space was also made for key Black historical figures, such as Equiano, Seacole and American civil rights campaigner Rosa Parks, and for a more critical engagement with issues around Empire and slavery.[13]

Why was this? Who made these decisions and to what end, if not for erasure of both identity and presence? If history does not record your name or tell your story, who will be able to argue in the future that you existed at all, that your people and culture mattered and still do? Inequality was embedded in the decision-making process around the development and publication of the new history curriculum in 2013/14 and, had it been allowed to have been published without revision, that inequality would have been embedded in the education system. As Syreeta Cumberbatch, from Black Cultural Archives, comments: 'Black students often don't recognise what they're taught at home as history; as the same as the academic discourse. They don't see their parents' stories in museums and galleries and archives, but when they see it there, they get excited about history.'[14] There are, of course, dedicated and impassioned teachers, working up and down the country to bring history alive and make it exciting to all *their* students. What those teachers need is support and empowerment, not boulders by government put in their way.

Secondary school history

Despite all debates around history, and the challenges and/or benefits of curriculum reform, learners are still very keen to study the subject at school:

> History remains a popular choice at both GCSE and A level, with a slight increase in entries for the June 2021 series at both stages. There are 278,880 provisional entries for GCSE history, and 41,585 entries for A-level history. Both of these figures represent a small increase on the previous year. Pupils who choose to study history at GCSE are likely to have at least 4 hours of history lessons per fortnight, although often they will have more history time than this. At A level, pupils are likely to have at least 8 hours of taught history lessons per fortnight.[15]

History is only available between years 7 and 9 (aged 11–14 or Key Stage 3). It does not have to be studied beyond this stage, as it is an option in most schools for GCSE. Yet, of course, it is not as clear cut as that because in some state schools it is pitted against other humanities subjects, such a geography. Further, limitations of the school timetable and resources mean that it may not be available to all students for further study beyond the age of 14.

History as a subject in schools is contentious and political not only in the UK. Think, for example, of the United States, where history does not exist in all states as a secondary school subject. Instead, it is taught as part of social studies. This means that the content and structure of what should be taught is even more fiercely debated by Americans at a local, federal and national level. Here in the England, we must also remember that the new history curriculum brought in by the Coalition Government was part of wider-scale reform across secondary education. There was a notion of restoration that permeated all subjects, not just history. Additionally:

> In relation to the curriculum there are four key moves within the agenda of restoration: the creation of the English Baccalaureate (E-Bac), the abolition of 'non-subjects', the specification of a secondary curriculum in some subjects and a new primary curriculum. The E-Bac is based on a traditional subject set (5+ GCSE A*–C grades including Maths, English, a science, a modern language and either History or Geography).[16]

The creation of the E-Bac was meant to also safeguard the position of subjects the government believe to be important. Yet there is also another explanation for this return to a traditional core of subjects:

> A different explanation for the call for a return to 'traditional' school history is advanced by educationalist Philip Beadle. Noting the high proportion of current cabinet ministers who themselves went to the most illustrious and traditionally inclined independent schools ('Robert Gordon, St Paul's,

Eton, Wellington, Rugby and Charterhouse...'),[17] he argues that this 'longing for the past' stems at least in part from the tendency of politicians to generalize from their own experiences of (traditional) education and their subsequent (successful) careers. The study of history at school thus becomes what one does before going up to Oxbridge, so to speak, for a political and social elite, rather than being considered in terms of what history might offer for 'ordinary people'. Beadle terms this 'My policies, based on my old schooldays'[18] and adds that 'As a basis for educational policy, reinstating and making universal your own experience is at best risibly unimpressive; at worst, it's a tissue-thin and profoundly unintelligent means of reinstating the perceived gap in quality between independent and state providers.'[19]

The reality, of course, is that the 'good old days' were only good for some, and that lived experience can be simultaneously shared and particular. The much-quoted words of British poet Damian Barr in relation to the global Covid-19 pandemic could also be used for so much of history: 'We are not all in the same boat. We are all in the same storm. Some of us are on super-yachts. Some have just the one oar.'[20]

Many educators will agree that history in schools cannot just be reduced to facts and learning by rote. The presence of the internet, formal and informal learning online, and access to more facts at our fingertips than ever before, means that the subject has to be more than information and knowledge acquisition. The subject has to develop both understanding, reflective skills and tools, and empathy:

> A 'connected narrative' requires little critical reflection beyond the trite rehearsal of received opinion. Additionally, the quality of empathy which history can evoke and foster is hardly encouraged by an 'island story' of kings, queens and prime ministers. Understanding that there were people in the past just like the students sitting in the classroom, with mothers and fathers, brothers and sisters, who had to make their way

in societies very different from those of the twenty-first century, demands an exercise of creative reconstruction that helps connect present and past in a more meaningful and immediate manner.[21]

History has the power to connect people, places and purposes across time, and catalyse agency. History can be made as well as read about, reviewed and analysed. In the flourishing of our children and young people there must be an active sense that history is not for them to receive passively. Rather, the subject calls for an active engagement of mind and body and heart. The Swann Report, published in 1985 'insisted on "Education for All" (DES 1985)' and 'recommended that "Britain is a multiracial and multicultural society and all pupils must be enabled to understand what this means" (1985, 770) ... The struggles over the History National Curriculum clearly illustrate how much is at stake and how much is still to achieve, in terms of recognition, policy and practice.'[22]

To sit on a bus freely as a Black British woman came at a price paid before I was born, a price paid from Bristol, UK to Montgomery, Alabama in the United States. To vote as a woman and as a Black woman meant that others had to participate and place all they had to review history and realize that the present had to respond in a different way. To be ordained priest meant that someone else had to recognize and stand firm, holding on to their place in history, whether it was Pauli Murray or Florence Li Tim-Oi or Rose-Hudson Wilkin or Lucy Winkett. History taught them one thing, but they challenged and lived out something else to make a new history. Yet, the sad truth is that:

> Of the 59 GCSE history modules available from the three biggest exam boards, Edexcel, AQA and OCR, 12 explicitly mention Black history. Only five mention the history of Black people in Britain, the rest are about Black people in the US, other countries or the transatlantic slave trade. Of the five that cover Black history in Britain, three include migration,

one deals with empire in the 17th and 18th century, and one mentions race relations in post-war Britain in a thematic study of power over an 850-year period. This means up to 11% (approx. 28,412) of GCSE students in 2019 were studying modules that made any reference to the contribution of Black people in British history.[23]

History of exclusion

Peoples and communities have always been excluded from history because a lot of the history we studied at school was often written by one demographic. Be it because of ethnicity (or the socially constructed notion of race), sex, gender, religion or beliefs, there are stories that we are never told about or that have not been placed in our school textbooks or favourite school resources.

In England, the 1971 seminal publication by Bernard Coard: 'How the West Indian Child is made Educationally Sub-Normal in the British School System'[24] made clear the inequalities and injustices of the education system at the time. For the first time, people could see how the system had been constructed to exclude as the book 'exposed many failings in the school system and galvanised parents and educationalists to look into alternative methods of education and led to the growth in Supplementary Schools'.[25]

This parallel education system, with its sub-normal schools, was explored by Black British film-maker, Steve McQueen in the fifth and final episode of his stunning anthology series *Small Axe* (2020), which focused on the fictional life of 12-year-old Kingsley Smith, and his journey through what was, in effect, a segregated education system in 1970s Britain. Coard's pamphlet energized the Black Education Movement, spawning the 'the Black Parents Movement – which lobbied for integration of ethnic minority and disabled children in schools, and established actively anti-racist "supplementary schools" for Black children'.[26]

PERIOD 8: HISTORY

McQueen, as executive producer, also worked with 'documentary maker Lyttanya Shannon, on *Subnormal*, a devastating documentary' which 'reveals how Britain's education system in the 60s and 70s was stacked against Black pupils – and still is today'.[27] Released in 2021, the label of 'subnormal' is interrogated:

> Her [documentary maker Lyttanya Shannon] focus was the Black British children who found themselves unfairly removed from mainstream education in the 1960s and 70s. They were sent to what were known as 'dustbin schools' – places for those deemed 'subnormal'. And Black children were four times as likely to be sent to them as white children. So raw was their pain, Shannon tells me, that it was hard to find anyone willing to discuss their time in such institutions on camera. '40 years on, the trauma was still very present,' she says.

This legacy of trauma and pain, as well as the practical consequences of missing out on the education offered to other children, was 'underpinned by eugenics and the belief that Black children were somehow lesser than white children.'[28] The tactics of separation, alienation and removing the ability to participate, all served to relegate Black children from mainstream education and treat them as second-class citizens. Further the absence of this and other parts of Black British history from the curriculum underlines a prevalent theme of erasure that only serves those who wish a superficial and homogenized view of history and of Britishness. As Shannon rightly notes:

> We all learn about the American civil rights movement and the resistance that took place there. Because we're not taught about those things in this country, we don't understand that there's a whole legacy of it here too – of Black intellectuals, Black educationists, Black parents, fighting for the rights of their children.[29]

The history teachers

Another key area of inequality relates to who is teaching history in our schools, and who is studying history in our universities, the prerequisite to obtaining your teaching qualification and certification.

> History teacher training faces particular issues around lack of diversity. In 2013, 543 students were accepted to study postgraduate teacher training courses specialising in history, but the proportion of successful Black and Minority Ethnic (BME) applicants was very low – only five Bangladeshi and four Pakistani descent students, and only two from Indian, Black African and mixed-race backgrounds. No Black Caribbean applicants were accepted. This lack of diversity is underpinned by a 'pipeline' issue, with comparatively small numbers of BME students learning history at University – only 8.7% of undergraduate students in history in 2012/13.[30] This, together with the often highly traditional and monocultural nature of these courses themselves, suggests that the future of history teaching is one in which BME individuals and perspectives simply do not feature.[31]

Of course, you do not have to be of global majority heritage to teach the history of these communities, but we know that representation matters. It is essential for children to see themselves reflected in the classroom and in school leadership, and in different power structures. This is a physical presentation that serves to deconstruct the 'victim and slave' narratives presented in a selective history curriculum.

The picture is no better at university level according to the Royal Historical Society's 2018 Report 'Race, Ethnicity & Equality in UK History':

> BME students and staff are underrepresented in UK History departments according to Advance HE's Equality Challenge Unit. This underrepresentation is particularly acute for Black students and staff.

PERIOD 8: HISTORY

- Historical & Philosophical Studies (H&PS) undergraduate student cohorts are overwhelmingly White, and have lower proportions of BME students (11.3%) than the overall UK undergraduate population (23.9%);
- BME representation in H&PS departments diminishes further at postgraduate level, with just 8.6% of H&PS UK postgraduate research students from BME backgrounds, compared to 16.8% of all UK postgraduate research students;
- History academic staff are less diverse than H&PS student cohorts, with 93.7% of History staff drawn from White backgrounds, and only 0.5% Black, 2.2% Asian and 1.6% Mixed.[32]

The report also presents the discrimination, bias and harassment faced by history students and staff based on their ethnicity. We can see that the talent pipeline is broken and so these statistics are unlikely to change unless there is active investment and intentional action at all levels of second and tertiary education. The government's own school workforce data, published in February 2021, reveals that

- In 2019, 85.7% of all teachers in state-funded schools in England were White British (where ethnicity was known)
- 78.5% of the working age population was White British at the time of the 2011 Census
- 3.8% of teachers were from the White Other ethnic group, the second highest percentage after the White British group
- 92.7% of headteachers were White British.[33]

It strikes me that our focus cannot simply be on the curriculum, but also the conditions in which it is taught and who is in charge of both designing and delivering that curriculum. Otherwise, we may find that the inequalities we seek to eradicate remain, but in myriad forms.

Reimagining history

How can history in schools promote and support the flourishing of children and young people? The Royal Historical Society notes 'the imperative need to widen taught History curriculums in schools and universities to challenge the racial foundations of the discipline and to reflect the full diversity of human histories'.[34] I have also pointed to the issue of who teaches history and in which contexts. Additionally, there is the external challenge of interference by government which, compared to other countries, can at times seem unusual:

> Whereas in many countries there has been a move towards using historical perspectives to develop young people's understanding of present-day issues and concerns, in the UK there has been a marked tendency for politicians and policymakers to try to limit the extent to which school history relates to present day issues.[35]

We cannot lose sight of the potential that history has to teach us how to live and relate better to each other as part of one human race. We cannot lose sight of the power of history to engender misunderstandings and falsehoods. We must invest in the purpose of history to bring us a deeper and broader understanding of how, as peoples, societies and communities we got to where we are today. As Bradley writes:

> History in schools should be a space in which children and young people can explore what it is to be human, through engaging with people's lives in other contexts. It should also teach them something about themselves and the people around them, and it should make people curious.[36]

If we were to reimagine history, it could be a subject studied through immersive experience with the choice of local, regional, national and international history available to all students. There would be the opportunity for students to create and develop projects through contextual discovery that speak to the location and milieu in which they are learning. It should be a challenge for students to find out about histories that have yet to be told and to work to build their evaluative and critical skills to unmask narratives that focus on misrepresentation and distortion. The ability to distinguish fact from opinion, the real from fake news, are skills that such a reimagination of the subject could develop.

Imagine a subject that comes alive through objects, places, text, film, audio recordings, song and dance, and that enables students to translate for themselves meaning that is linked to their own lived experience and that of their families. Imagine a subject that gives students the tools to read present issues with the historic antecedents in mind. A five-dimensional approach, that explores history through people, place (natural and human-made), objects and materials, cultural production and identity would open new conversations and new ways to engage with the past as well as the present. Five-dimensional history offers different ways for learners to connect with themes and topics and to build links between them.

Notes

1 Lloyd Bowen, Kate Bradley, Simon Middleton, et al., 2012, 'History in the UK National Curriculum: A Discussion', *Cultural and Social History*, 9(1), pp. 125–43, p. 138.

2 Lord Palmerston, 1858. This extract from his address can be found in the foyer of the National Portrait Gallery, London, cited in Terry Haydn, 2012, '"Longing for the Past": Politicians and the History Curriculum in English Schools, 1988–2010', *Journal of Educational Media, Memory, and Society*, 4(1), p. 22.

3 Haydn, '"Longing for the Past": Politicians and the History Curriculum', p. 9.

4 Haydn, '"Longing for the Past": Politicians and the History Curriculum', p. 10.

5 Bowen, Bradley, Middleton, et al., 'History in the UK National Curriculum', p. 127.

6 Bowen, Bradley, Middleton, et al., 'History in the UK National Curriculum', p. 128.

7 Haydn, '"Longing for the Past": Politicians and the History Curriculum', p. 12.

8 Robert Guyver, 2016, 'England and the UK: Conflict and Consensus over Curriculum' in Robert Guyver (ed.), *Teaching History and the Changing Nation State: Transnational and Intranational Perspectives*, London: Bloomsbury Academic, pp. 159–74, http://dx.doi.org/10.5040/9781474225892.ch-009, accessed 31.08.2020.

9 Stephen J. Ball, 2017, *The Education Debate*, Bristol: Polity Press, p. 105.

10 Claire Alexander and Debbie Weekes-Bernard, 2012, 'Making British Histories: Diversity and the National Curriculum', London: Runnymede Trust.

11 Claire Alexander and Debbie Weekes-Bernard, 2017, 'History Lessons: Inequality, Diversity and the National Curriculum', *Race, Ethnicity and Education*, 20(4), pp. 478–94, p. 482.

12 Operation Black Vote, www.obv.org.uk/

13 Alexander and Weekes-Bernard, 'History Lessons', p. 483.

14 Alexander and Weekes-Bernard, 'History Lessons', p. 485.

15 Ofsted, 2021, 'Research review series: history', *Gov.uk*, 14 July, www.gov.uk/government/publications/research-review-series-history, accessed 01.03.2022.

16 Ball, *The Education Debate*, pp. 106.

17 Phillip Beadle, 2011, 'The English Bac and the Status Quo', *Education Guardian*, 26 April, p. 5.

18 Phillip Beadle, 2011, 'My Policies, Based on my Old School Days', *Education Guardian*, 4 January, p. 5.

19 Haydn, '"Longing for the Past": Politicians and the History Curriculum', p. 16.

20 Damian Barr, 'We are not all in the same boat', *Damien Barr*, www.damianbarr.com/latest/https/we-are-not-all-in-the-same-boat, accessed 01.03.2022.

21 Bowen, Bradley, Middleton, et al., 'History in the UK National Curriculum', p. 132.

22 Alexander and Weekes-Bernard, 'History Lessons', p. 490.

23 Anna Leach, Antonio Voce and Ashley Kirk, 2020, 'Black British history: the row over the school curriculum in England', *The Guardian*, 13 July, www.theguardian.com/education/2020/jul/13/black-british-history-school-curriculum-england, accessed 01.03.2022.

24 Bernard Coard, 1971, *How the West Indian Child is Made Educationally Sub-normal in the British School System*, London: New Beacon for the Caribbean Education and Community Workers' Association.

PERIOD 8: HISTORY

25 Black Cultural Archives, *Education Subject Guide*, 2016, https://static1.squarespace.com/static/5a01baa7d7bdcee985c80c15/t/5a0891be41920291507c4d2f/1510511040225/2016_Education-updated.pdf, accessed 01.03.2022.

26 Micha Frazer-Carroll, 2021, '"Black kids were written off": the scandal of the children sent to "dustbin schools"', *The Guardian*, 19 May, www.theguardian.com/tv-and-radio/2021/may/19/black-kids-were-written-off-the-scandal-of-the-children-sent-to-dustbin-schools, accessed 01.03.2022.

27 Frazer-Carroll, '"Black kids were written off"'.

28 Frazer-Carroll, '"Black kids were written off"'.

29 Frazer-Carroll, '"Black kids were written off"'.

30 Indeed, only 1.9% of historical and philosophical studies students were Black and 2.5% British Asian; Higher Education Statistics Agency (HESA) Student Introduction 2012/13, www.hesa.ac.uk/stats, cited in Alexander and Weekes-Bernard, 'History Lessons', p. 491.

31 Alexander and Weekes-Bernard, 'History Lessons', p. 489.

32 Royal Historical Society, 2018, *Race, Ethnicity & Equality in UK History: A Report and Resource for Change*, October, p. 8.

33 UK Government, 2021, 'School Teacher Workforce', *Gov.uk*, 18 February www.ethnicity-facts-figures.service.gov.uk/workforce-and-business/workforce-diversity/school-teacher-workforce/latest#:~:text=Percentage%20and%20number%20of%20school%20teachers%20by%20ethnicity,%20%207%2C200%20%2019%20more%20rows%20, accessed 01.03.2022.

34 Royal Historical Society, *Race, Ethnicity & Equality in UK History*, p. 10.

35 Haydn, '"Longing for the Past": Politicians and the History Curriculum', p. 8.

36 Bowen, Bradley, Middleton, et al., 'History in the UK National Curriculum', p. 131.

Period 9: Maths

Calculating the Cost

> He entered Jericho and was passing through it. A man was there named Zacchaeus; he was a chief tax-collector and was rich. He was trying to see who Jesus was, but on account of the crowd he could not, because he was short in stature. So he ran ahead and climbed a sycamore tree to see him, because he was going to pass that way. When Jesus came to the place, he looked up and said to him, 'Zacchaeus, hurry and come down; for I must stay at your house today.' So he hurried down and was happy to welcome him. All who saw it began to grumble and said, 'He has gone to be the guest of one who is a sinner.' Zacchaeus stood there and said to the Lord, 'Look, half of my possessions, Lord, I will give to the poor; and if I have defrauded anyone of anything, I will pay back four times as much.' Then Jesus said to him, 'Today salvation has come to this house, because he too is a son of Abraham. For the Son of Man came to seek out and to save the lost.'
> (Luke 19.1–10)

The fact that those who defraud can afford to pay back the defrauded four times the original amount, and still have something left over, highlights the persistent nature of inequality in our world. There needs to be a recognition, first, that there is enough for all to share and, second, that monetary wealth bears no relation to the state of the soul or the peace of individuals and or communities. We all have a calling to leave the world in a better state than that into which we were born.

There is a contrast of perspectives between the man up in the tree and the people walking alongside Jesus. The crowds

PERIOD 9: MATHS

pressed in on hope, and light, and truth. The crowds needed the time, space and opportunity to talk about freedom and opportunity. They needed who they were as a people and as individuals, and their potential, to be recognized and underlined. The financially secure and assured also needed something of this recognition of potential. And this was what Jesus saw, as he always did, the potential in this wealthy man, who already knew that his portion had been excess and greed. The admonishment is not necessary. The fact that Jesus asks Zacchaeus to come down from the tree has metaphorical as well as literal weight. Zacchaeus knows how to redress the balance and establish equity once more. This is an encounter that transforms, and he chooses a better path.

The maths needs to add up so there is more than sufficient provision for all. This means better access to resources and better access to opportunities. Putting profits before human flourishing results in a damaging and prevalent legacy of disenfranchisement. The gap between rich and poor has always been recognized by those who suffer and live the consequences of uneven distribution, a lack of care, and sometimes intentional distancing between those who have and those who do not. This gap has not always been recognized by those who caused these consequences. And this is what needs to happen for structural and systemic change to occur.

Everyone has a part to play in co-creating the world we wish to see and in which we seek to live more equitable lives. The economic, social, health and political disequilibria in which few thrive, and in which poverty becomes a bedrock, only serves a minority. Poverty is not inevitable, human rights are not optional, and human potential is not limited to the few. The maths of resourcing opportunity and access, of ensuring and safeguarding equity needs to add up.

***

Quadratic equations. That was the only class test in which I scored 100 per cent in maths. I am not sure what happened because I was as shocked as the superstar mathematicians in my class. I am still proud of that class test, and probably have it somewhere in the box of secondary school work in my garage. The pride, over the years, has waned as maths is a subject I left behind at GCSE, having completed my exam a year early. This gave me more free time in Year 11 and more breathing space. I was never enamoured by maths, having never being told I was good at it or that I could be good at it but clearly when I put my mind to it, it clicked. Now I work for a charity that focuses on chemistry education, the gauntlet has been gently laid down for me to complete a GCSE in the subject in the near future. I hope that those who generously make the time to read this book will keep me in their prayers for this Everest-like challenge.

The reality for me is that maths was always about confidence. My gift was language, or at least I felt so, thus I just felt like an impostor every time we had maths class and the resulting homework. I always did this homework and I always made sure that I took my time to understand it properly. But I can't remember any female maths teachers, though I know from my classmates that girls could be brilliant at maths. That was the richness of being in a girls' school. What, pray tell, could girls not do exactly? Now, I am older and, dare I hope, wiser, I'd love to take up maths again, knowing what I know now, that the voice in my head was a combination of no external affirmation and interior chaos of teenage hormones and illogical deselection. So, when I read in January 2020 that all 30 students in a class at Fitzalan High School in Cardiff, Wales, had achieved A* in their maths GCSE because of their committed maths teacher, Mr Francis Elive, known as the 'maths whisperer', I completely understood what this meant. As the headteacher stated, 'he instils the belief that they have practised the hardest maths that they have to ever to face so why be scared of an exam? It's the belief that they absolutely can do it, and the children think it's magic.'[1] We should never underestimate the power of our belief in our children and young people.

PERIOD 9: MATHS

Maths anxiety

In August 2021, a national newspaper stated the following:

> Amid the celebrations by students getting their A-level and GCSE results this week, it almost passed without notice that girls had stormed the last bastion of male academic attainment by capturing more top grades in maths than boys in both qualifications.[2]

This follows decades of research that detailed the gender inequality across maths and science subjects. There is still, nevertheless, ongoing research into maths anxiety:

> Maths anxiety (MA) is a negative emotional response to a current or prospective situation involving mathematics. The effects of MA are educationally debilitating; MA sufferers have decreased maths self-confidence, enjoy maths less and may even avoid maths altogether ...
>
> Nevertheless, the majority of studies have investigated MA in university and secondary school samples; MA research employing primary and early secondary school populations remains surprisingly sparse ...[3]

The cohort used by these researchers 'consisted of 1014 children attending both primary and secondary schools in Italy'.[4] With the increase in the achievement of girls, it would be easy to discount or dismiss MA, but this would be short-sighted. How much MA affects children in the UK, particularly during clear moments of transition in the education system (for example, primary to secondary school) merits further research. What is clear is that there was some evidence of a correlation between MA and the identity of the students:

> Firstly, our results indicate that girls have greater MA than boys, corroborating findings from studies on adult, secondary and primary samples. Importantly, this gender difference

was found in both our primary and secondary cohorts. Our data demonstrate that differences in boys' and girls' MA can emerge early in primary school. We found no gender difference in maths performance. Secondly, whilst we found a stable negative relationship between MA and maths performance in secondary students, this relationship was not reliable in primary students. The negative MA/maths performance link thus appears to surface later in the educational timeline, perhaps as a result of the greater demands associated with the secondary maths curriculum. This signals the need for the development of measures aimed at halting MA's emergence in primary school.[5]

From our national perspective, however, it is important to also hold on to the fact that 'after a significant drop in the number of students taking Maths A-Level in 2019, we have seen the student population rise by over 2,000 students in 2020. The proportion of girls taking A-Level Maths has remained stable.'[6] In 2019, 35,605 girls took maths at A level, which rose to 37,103 in 2020, 39 per cent of the total number of entrants across both years.[7] Maths is an obligatory subject at GCSE. At A level, the numbers indicate a choice by girls to continue with the subject at this higher level.

The Maths National Curriculum (MNC)

If we return to maths pre-16, we see that the subject has suffered the same fate as other subjects in terms of its creation and then (constant) revision:

> The mathematics NC was first introduced in 1989 and was revised in 1991 and again in 1995. The implementation of the latest version (1999) of the mathematics NC in 2000 followed a five-year period of no change. During this period, the QCA monitored the impact of the curriculum and consulted widely about potential changes. The work of two Royal

PERIOD 9: MATHS

Society/Joint Mathematical Council working groups was a significant influence on the curriculum changes.[8]

There was another revision in 2013, published the following year, this time with three aims for all pupils:

- become fluent in the fundamentals of mathematics, including through varied and frequent practice with increasingly complex problems over time, so that pupils develop conceptual understanding and the ability to recall and apply knowledge rapidly and accurately
- reason mathematically by following a line of enquiry, conjecturing relationships and generalisations, and developing an argument, justification or proof using mathematical language
- can solve problems by applying their mathematics to a variety of routine and non-routine problems with increasing sophistication, including breaking down problems into a series of simpler steps and persevering in seeking solutions.[9]

This is what all teachers are ultimately working towards in terms of what their students should be able to do by the end of their school years. It may be useful to highlight that at GCSE level there are two tiers. Schools select which students do which tier, which may of course lead to some students being precluded from entering for the higher tier:

> For those less familiar with the detail of GCSE maths, there are two tiers: foundation and higher. Each tier is targeted at a range of the new numerical grades: 9 to 4 on the higher tier (with a 'safety net' grade 3 for students scoring a small number of marks below grade 4), and 5 to 1 on the foundation tier.
>
> Students can achieve grades 5 to 3 on both tiers, and the exam papers will include some questions that are the same on both tiers. This will help exam boards ensure that it is no more or less difficult to achieve the same grade on different tiers.[10]

As a point of reference, a new grading system was introduced in 2014:

> The numerical grading scheme is part of a curriculum introduced in England's schools in 2014 by then Education Secretary Michael Gove. GCSE courses now include much less coursework than before, with grades in almost all subjects depending on exams. This has not been the case in 2020 and 2021, when the end-of-year public exams were cancelled. Courses are designed to be more challenging, with exams taken after two years of study rather than in modules with exams along the way.[11]

Thus we have:[12]

Old grades	New grades
A*	9
	8
A	7
B	6
	5 STRONG PASS
C	4 STANDARD PASS
D	3
E	
F	2
G	1
U	U

There is no transparent process for how schools allocate students to each tier, meaning of course that this will be down to a combination of teachers, heads of department and sometimes the senior leadership team (SLT) to decide. There is also no research to reveal if there are any prevalent inequalities in this regard across England, an investigation that needs to be done to ensure equal access to opportunities. If a particular group of students are not encouraged or even allowed to enter the higher tier for mathematics there should be good, justifiable and visible reasons for this, as the highest grade that can be obtained in the foundation tier is 5, limiting any future opportunity to progress to study maths at advanced level.

There are greater questions, too, about what the study of maths is for in society. As John Westwell reminds us:

> The role of mathematics education in our society is complex. There is no simple consensus as to which mathematics is important or how it should be taught. Indeed, there is controversy about the nature of mathematics itself. Different social groups have influenced and will continue to influence the shape of mathematics education. Mathematics teachers experience the influence of such groups through their teaching associations, curriculum projects, recommendations of official reports and government policy on curriculum and assessment.[13]

As with all subjects, there has to be room for the study of maths for maths' sake, exploring the subject for its beauty and internal coherency, as well as maths in its applied forms. What is essential for us as a society is that we sufficiently invest in the provision, opportunities and access to mathematics for all children.

Funding for schools

In thinking about maths, the key question also has to be: do the figures add up in terms of investment in our schools and the educators within them? The simple answer is no. In 2001, an article in the *Times Education Supplement* bemoaned the

INEQUALITY AND FLOURISHING

disparity in funding between primary and secondary schools across the UK:

> 'The bias has always been to support the secondary schools and the small primaries, which have a huge lobby,' says Jenny Davies, head of Westborough school in Southend, Essex (760 on roll). 'No one has ever been able to justify to me why secondaries get a bigger budget.'[14]

It remains unclear why primary schools with equal number of students to some secondary schools do not receive the same amount of funding. This has a direct impact on amplifying educational inequalities:

> 'There are equal opportunities issues here,' says Frank Gulley, head at Temple Sutton primary, Southend, with 770 on roll. 'There's no recognition of the management structure you need to have. I have one non-teaching deputy head. In a similar secondary school, there would be three deputies, plus heads of year – all with additional non-contact time. I have no lab assistants, no information communications technology technician, no bursar, no reprographics staff'.[15]

In essence we have an education system with some parts better funded than others, without due recognition of the impact on teachers, students and the wider community. The government at the time, however, wanted to ensure that they set the record straight, but this only amplified the reality of the challenge primary school leaders were facing:

> The Department for Education and Skills says that small secondaries receive approximately 50 per cent more money than a comparable primary. 'This is largely due to the need to provide a full curriculum through specialist teachers,' said a spokesperson. But primary heads say the real figure is closer to double the funding for an equivalent secondary.[16]

PERIOD 9: MATHS

Fast forward 19 years and, in 2020, the government wanted to make sure that everyone knew it was increasing spending on education:

> The total amount of funding allocated to English schools for 5–16-year-old pupils has grown since 2010–11 as the total pupil population has grown. In cash terms, the total funding allocated to schools through the grants covered in this report was £47.6 billion in 2020–21, an increase of 36.1% compared to the £35 billion allocated in 2010–11, and is increasing to £49.6 billion in 2021–22. On a per-pupil basis the total funding allocated to schools for 5–16-year-old pupils, in cash terms, in 2020–21 was £6,280, a 21.3% increase compared to £5,180 allocated per pupil in 2010–11.[17]

Yet against the backdrop of the pandemic, scrutiny meant that these figures did not seem as laudable as they first appeared. The truth of the matter is that our state schools are still underfunded, and this means teachers and school leaders often have to work under added pressure to deliver when the resources simply are not there:

> The Department for Education's (the Department's) total funding for mainstream schools increased from £36.2 billion in 2014–15 to £43.4 billion in 2020–21. However, the increase in pupil numbers meant real-terms funding per pupil rose by only 0.4%. The Department plans to increase school funding in 2021–22 and 2022–23, so total and per-pupil funding is expected to rise in real terms by around 4%. However, the Department did not take account of the potential impact of COVID-19 as part of its assessment of cost pressures. While the Department provided schools with funding during the early stages of the pandemic for exceptional costs, and later in 2020 to help schools cover costs arising from staff absences, several stakeholders told the NAO [National Audit Office] that this funding would be insufficient.[18]

You cannot expect a house to be warm without windows, a door or a roof. The financial impact of the pandemic has not been recognized by the government. This is a failure to recognize the responsibility towards this current and next generation of learners. It is impossible to believe that the government has no money for education when it awarded a ridiculous amount of money for contracts for personal protective equipment (PPE) that were ineffective, out of date or never used.[19] This was a colossal waste of public funds, which could clearly have been better spent.

A new funding formula for schools was introduced in 2018–19, but this has only served to increase the educational inequalities already evident in the allocation of money to schools:

> It allocates three-quarters of school funding based on pupil numbers, and the remainder is based on factors relating to the characteristics of pupils and schools ... As part of the national funding formula, the Department introduced a new minimum per-pupil funding arrangement. In 2020–21, the levels were set at £3,750 per primary pupil and £5,000 per secondary pupil. Under the minimum funding arrangement, 37% of the least deprived fifth of schools were allocated more funding in 2020–21. However, none of the most deprived fifth of schools were allocated an increase in funding as a result of this arrangement. This is because these schools were already receiving per-pupil funding above the new minimum requirement.

So, while it could be argued that more funding has been given to the schools most in need, we note that the reality is that 'between 2017–18 and 2020–21, average per-pupil funding in the most deprived fifth of schools fell in real terms by 1.2%, while per-pupil funding in the least deprived fifth increased by 2.9%. In total, 58.3% of the most deprived fifth of schools saw a real-terms decrease in per-pupil funding'.[20]

PERIOD 9: MATHS

This and every government needs to move from piling on the pressure on schools and their educators to piling on the monetary pounds to ensure that adequate funds can be allocated to our schools, for the sake of our children, their potential and their flourishing.

The pupil premium

We need to talk, too, about the pupil premium, what it is, why it is there and how it is used.

> The Pupil Premium was introduced by the Coalition Government in April 2011 for children of low-income families, eligible for free school meals (FSM) or who had been 'looked after' continuously for more than 6 months. It also included those children from families with parents in the Armed Forces. From April 2012 funding was extended to include children who had been eligible for FSM at any point in the last 6 years – the Ever 6 measure ... The funding was additional to the school budget and was intended to be used specifically to close the attainment gap between pupils who were eligible for the funding and the attainment of their peers who were not entitled for the additional funding.[21]

The pupil premium aims to alleviate some of the educational inequalities detailed in this book, with the focus being on attainment. It can add substantially to a school budget especially if the school has a high number of students in receipt of FSM:

> The amount of funding received by an individual school with high FSM, particularly if it is a large school, can be considerable. There is evidence that since the introduction of Pupil Premium funding, schools have encouraged families to register for FSM and, while acknowledging they may have undertaken to do so anyway, schools nevertheless have informed

parents that registering for FSM will increase the funding received by their school.[22]

We have already talked about FSM in earlier chapters and the need to ensure and expand their provision. It is important to reflect here that the pupil premium funding can be a lifeline for schools, offering additional resources to ensure equality of access and provision to support learning, and of opportunities (for example, to attend school trips) beyond school:

> For the 2017/18 academic year, children who have received FSM in the last six years receive £1,320 for primary and £935 for secondary; children who are or were looked after (i.e. in Local Authority care) receive £1,900; and children of armed forces personnel receive £300. By far the largest group is those in receipt of FSM. To be eligible for FSM (and hence the pupil premium) a child's parents must be receiving one of a listed number of (largely out of work) benefits.[23]

Nevertheless, it is also crucial to note that the metrics by which schools are judged on the impact of their pupil premium funding is limiting, focusing on attainment in English and maths. This does not take into account the range of measures that school leaders and teachers may need to put in place to ensure that a child or young person can actually engage with school and learning in the first place. It is clear that 'there is real pressure on headteachers and teachers to reconcile the demands of meeting the needs of individual students and meeting externally imposed targets'.[24] Schools, guided by the decisions of the senior leadership team will decide how best to use this designated funding often encountering a conflict between the legal and the moral imperative of support some vs all students, and also of deciding what intervention would best serve the whole education of the students under their care. Due to the cuts to external services and support, and the existing socio-economic challenges that manifest in schools, pupil premium funding may be used by some schools to simply plug the gap for provision that should have been there in the first place:

PERIOD 9: MATHS

> Funding to work with children for focused support for counselling or mentoring to enhance well-being or reduce or remove barriers to learning are common strategies ... Many schools often used external providers such as advisers or educational psychologists to improve behaviour or attendance. Ofsted (2012)[25] found that these strategies were funded to a lesser extent than those used to pay for teachers to target underperformance, particularly in English and Maths. Other expenditure included subsidies for educational visits or the purchase of uniform and equipment (Ofsted, 2012).[26]

Funding for Special Education Needs and Disability (SEND)

> In 2019 there were 354,000 children and young people with education, health and care (EHC) plans or statements. These set out the support a child with SEND (special educational needs and disability) should receive, funded through local councils.[27]

I could not write this chapter without mentioning the clear and present injustice of chronic underfunding for students with special educational needs and disabilities. Whatever your political colours, no one could argue that we have an education system, whether now or in the past, that has served SEND students well. Each generation has attempted to create better models, to engage in the debate around inclusive education and to right the terrible wrongs of how students with additional needs have been treated. This is educational inequality writ large, and it continues to remain as a collective and a social indictment.

The Local Government Association campaign 'Bright Futures' is clear that those who will suffer are the children and young people who need the most help. They have called on the government 'to invest an additional £1.6 billion in high needs funding for SEND by 2021/22'.[28] This is the shortfall they have calculated due to increased demand and years of underfunding. The message to government was also boldly stated in the LGA Briefing to the House of Commons in January 2020:

> More children with special needs are now being educated outside of mainstream schools. SEND statistics show that 52 per cent of the 271,165 children and young people with Education, Health and Care Plans (EHCPs) were placed in state special schools, alternative provision, or independent and non-maintained special schools in 2019. This is impacting on council budgets due to the higher costs associated with placements in maintained special schools and independent or non-maintained special schools.[29]

In essence the trend appears to be that there is no incentive to keep children and young people with EHCPs in mainstream education. Schools are not rewarded or celebrated for an inclusive approach. Ofsted inspections also do not interrogate schools on their students with ECHPs and the provision for their flourishing:

> Rather than focussing primarily on academic results, Ofsted should also place more emphasis on how schools ensure an inclusive environment for children with SEND, as part of their new inspection framework. They must also hold to account schools with low numbers of children with SEND.[30]

All of this means that our education system becomes even less integrated and more exclusive. Children with ECHPs are treated differently (this does not necessarily mean positively in all cases) and set apart because the structures, funding and resources in place (or not, as the case may be) do not serve them. There is no sense that schools as they are currently set up were ever designed to meet their needs:

> An LGA commissioned report on SEND found that a combination of funding constraints, accountability pressures

PERIOD 9: MATHS

and curriculum changes in mainstream schools have reduced capacity to make available good quality provision for children with SEND ... Placing a child in a special school is significantly more expensive than a mainstream education.[31]

In some cases, a special school may be the best and most nurturing environment for a student with an EHCP, yet:

> The average annual cost to a council of a special needs placement in 2017/18, was £6,000 per pupil per year in a mainstream school, compared with £23,000 per pupil per year in a maintained special school, and £40,000 per pupil per year in an independent or non-maintained special school.[32]

The consequences of a lack of financial support to better provide for students with SEND means that these particular students have little to no chance of flourishing and are relegated to being second class citizens:

> We are concerned that unless additional funding is made available, councils will not be able to meet their statutory duties to support children and young people with Special Educational Needs and Disabilities.[33]

Why should the life and educational chances of students with SEND be hindered or curtailed because they have additional needs? What does that say about us as a society? We need to be angry about this because we cannot judge ourselves on how well our independent and selective schools are doing if we are ignoring the potential of students with SEND in our mainstream state schools. Many parents and carers of children with SEND will be able to detail their fights to get support for their child, support which has been directly and often negatively affected by the pandemic. They cannot be fighting alone without pressure on this and successive governments to do more and to be held accountable to these children. There are approximately 400,000 children waiting for us to getting angry enough to make the change that we want to see happen.

Reimagining mathematics

It is time to get our priorities right as a nation. Of course, not everyone is a parent and not everyone knows or supports a learner with SEND. Yet, my hope is that we can find common ground in the realization that if children suffer, we as a society suffer. We pay for the fact that we let them down. Mathematics is more than what happens in the classroom or how the curriculum is constructed and deconstructed. It is about how numbers make us see something new, patterns and correlation and beauty, how numbers offer proofs and how also they can be interpreted and misinterpreted.

We need to reimagine mathematics in and beyond the classroom; in the classroom as a subject that can surprise and delight, and be presented as a subject for all. We need more maths teachers who reflect the communities in which they teach, with more female role models celebrated from the past and the present across all ethnicities and backgrounds. Is there another model for testing mathematical understanding that is not a GCSE which separates students into foundation and higher tiers?

Beyond the classroom, maths could be offered continuously as a community-based course which focused on empowerment and purpose and application. Reimagining the pupil premium measured against deeper outcomes as well as outputs would liberate schools from the current reductive measurements. It is important to remain accountable so the funds are used wisely and appropriately, but it is also crucial to see how these funds could best serve the children in terms of holistic, whole-child education.

Finally, funding for schools cannot be seen as an afterthought with tokenistic announcements that belie the seriousness of the current education landscape and financial situations schools are facing. We need to reimagine all funding for education as an investment with the highest of returns, the flourishing of *all* our children and young people. Children and young people with SEND, therefore, should be seen as offering opportunities to devise new creative and imaginative inclusive solutions that have dignity at their core. We need a dignified financial response to educational provision for students with ECHPs, that neither belittles nor ignores, that champions their education as part of, not excluded from, the whole.

Notes

1 Sally Weale, 2020, '"Maths whisperer": Cardiff teacher gets A* grades for entire class', *The Guardian*, 22 January, www.theguardian.com/education/2020/jan/22/maths-whisperer-cardiff-teacher-francis-elive-gets-a-grades-for-entire-class, accessed 01.03.2022.

2 Richard Adams, 2021, 'Girls overtake boys in A-level and GCSE maths, so are they "smarter"?', *The Guardian*, 13 August, www.theguardian.com/education/2021/aug/13/girls-overtake-boys-in-a-level-and-gcse-maths-so-are-they-smarter, accessed 01.03.2022.

3 Francesca Hill, Irene C. Mammarella, Amy Devine, Sara Caviola, et al., 2016, 'Maths anxiety in primary and secondary school students: Gender differences, developmental changes and anxiety specificity', *Learning and Individual Differences* 48, pp. 45–53, p. 45.

4 Hill, Mammarella, Devine, Caviola, et al., 'Maths anxiety in primary and secondary school students', p. 47.

5 Hill, Mammarella, Devine, Caviola, et al., 'Maths anxiety in primary and secondary school students', p. 51.

6 Wise, 2020, 'Analysis Of 2020 A-Level Core STEM Entrants – Number Of Core STEM* A-Levels Completed By Girls Rises Again', *Wise*, www.wisecampaign.org.uk/statistics/analysis-of-2020-a-level-core-stem-entrants-number-of-core-stem-a-levels-completed-by-girls-rises-again/, accessed 01.03.2022.

7 Wise, 'Analysis Of 2020 A-Level Core STEM Entrants'.

8 John Westwell, 2010, 'Maths Education – Who Decides?' in Sue Johnston-Wilder, Clare Lee, David Pimm (eds) (3rd edn), *Learning to Teach Mathematics in the Secondary School: A Companion to School Experience*, London: Routledge, pp. 6–20, p. 26.

9 Department for Education, 2014, *Mathematics Programmes of Study: key stage 4*, July, p. 3.

10 Cath Jadhav, 2017, 'GCSE maths: choosing the "right" tier', *The*

Ofqual Blog, 10 February, https://ofqual.blog.gov.uk/2017/02/10/gcse-maths-choosing-the-right-tier/, accessed 01.03.2022.

11 BBC News, 2021, 'GCSEs 2021: The 9-1 grading system explained', 12 August, www.bbc.co.uk/news/education-48993830?at_medium=RSS&at_campaign=KARANGA, accessed 01.03.2022.

12 BBC News, 2021, 'GCSEs 2021: The 9-1 grading system explained', 12 August, www.bbc.co.uk/news/education-48993830?at_medium=RSS&at_campaign=KARANGA, accessed 01.03.2022

13 Westwell, 'Maths Education – Who Decides?', p. 19.

14 Phil Revell, 2001, 'Big roll does not equal big money', *TES*, 23 November.

15 Revell, 'Big roll does not equal big money'.

16 Revell, 'Big roll does not equal big money'.

17 UK Government, 2021, *Financial Year 2020–21 School funding statistics*, 28 January, https://explore-education-statistics.service.gov.uk/find-statistics/school-funding-statistics/2020-21, accessed 01.03.2022.

18 National Audit Office, 2021, *School Funding in England*, 2 July, states, 'A report by the Education Policy Institute, "Assessing Covid-19 cost pressures on England's schools", in December 2020 estimated that the Department's additional funding met 3 of the costs incurred by schools because of the pandemic from March to November 2020. The NAO also consulted the following stakeholders: the Association of Directors of Children's Services; the Association of School and College Leaders; the County Councils Network; the Institute of School Business Leadership and the Confederation of School Trusts; the Local Government Association; the National Association of Head Teachers; the National Education Union; the National Foundation for Educational Research; NASUWT, The Teachers' Union; and Parentkind', www.nao.org.uk/press-release/school-funding-in-england/, accessed 01.03.2022.

19 BMJ, 2021, 'The UK's PPE procurement scandal reminds us why we need ways to hold ministers to account', www.bmj.com/content/372/bmj.n639, accessed 06.04.2022.

20 National Audit Office, *School Funding in England*.

21 Ian Abbott, David Middlewood, Sue Robinson, 2015, 'It's not just about value for money: A case study of values-led implementation of the Pupil Premium in outstanding schools', *Management in Education*, 29(4), pp. 178–84, p. 178.

22 Abbott, Middlewood and Robinson, 'It's not just about value for money', p. 179.

23 David Barrett, 2018, 'The effective design, implementation and enforcement of socio-economic equality duties: lessons from the pupil premium', *Journal of Social Welfare and Family Law*, 40(1), pp. 57–77, p. 62.

24 Abbott, Middlewood and Robinson, 'It's not just about value for money', p. 179.

25 Ofsted, 2012, *The Pupil Premium: How schools are using the Pupil Premium funding to raise achievement for disadvantaged pupils.*

26 Abbott, Middlewood and Robinson, 'It's not just about value for money', p. 182.

27 Local Government Association, 'Bright Futures: SEND funding', *Local Government Association*, www.local.gov.uk/about/campaigns/bright-futures/bright-futures-childrens-services/bright-futures-send-funding, accessed 01.03.2022.

28 Local Government Association, 'Bright Futures: SEND funding'.

29 Local Government Association Briefing, 2020, 'Special Educational Needs and Disability Funding', *House of Commons*, 29 January, p. 1.

30 Local Government Association Briefing, 'Special Educational Needs and Disability Funding', p. 3.

31 Local Government Association Briefing, 'Special Educational Needs and Disability Funding', p. 2.

32 Local Government Association Briefing, 'Special Educational Needs and Disability Funding', p. 3.

33 Local Government Association Briefing, 'Special Educational Needs and Disability Funding', p. 1.

Towards a New Vision for Secondary Education

In this book I have argued for a more coherent education system that serves all children, and which invests in the potential and flourishing of each child. I have not been able to cover all of secondary education and I am acutely aware that there was no room for a robust discussion about vocational qualifications, the incredible work of FE Colleges and their staff, or whether university should be presented as the only route for all children. There also has not been the space to discuss the effects of provision (or lack of) on different demographics using an intersectional lens, which would also merit further interrogation. Last, I have not had the opportunity to delve into the education systems of Wales, Scotland and Northern Ireland, with the points of convergence and divergence that such an investigation would bring. As my experience has been in the English system, it was solid ground, from which hopefully I can conduct further research in the future.

As I conclude this book, my feeling that a new vision for secondary education in England is needed has not diminished. We need a reorientated, child-centred education that focuses on the whole person and gives equal access to opportunities and learning. There needs to be a realization by government that cuts have an impact and just because you may not be sending your own child to the local school, that does not make it acceptable. More funding is needed across all levels of education and especially for SEND provision. Schools cannot be held at the mercy of contracts that impoverish the school site, and the dignity of every child must be upheld and safeguarded.

TOWARDS A NEW VISION

Schools also cannot stand in isolation from the community, but should be part of a co-creative process of empowerment and agency-building, to enable the community to be what it seeks to be:

> Gunter[1] has commented about the importance of schools being involved in their local community and the development of 'a place-based curriculum that enables education to be directly involved in regeneration, where children are educated to want to build the community rather than leave it'.[2]

Of course, it is fundamental that schools must be safe, and should safeguard the physical and mental well-being of every child. They should also be part of the community; living, breathing and reflecting the human story of the people who live near and around the school, and those who commute to work and study there. Finally, we need to free our children from the intellectual and creative straightjackets of public exams and the shaming and labelling that comes with them:

> There has been a consistent irony in the unfolding of the last 30 years of curriculum making in England. On the one hand, government has reduced curriculum specification and has very visibly given schools, academies and free schools, greater curriculum autonomy. The motif is about freedoms from control. On the other hand, governments, of all parties, have retained control over schools and the school curriculum through the intense focus on exam and test results.[3]

With these fundamental principles, a new vision for secondary education can be built using a ten-point manifesto:

1. Learning does not start or stop at the school gates. It is time to review the school day and the school year. Long summer vacations are not helpful for all children. Is there a way for schools to be open all year round for different purposes and with different staffing?

2. Citizenship is not about exclusion. Rather it is about ensuring that democracy is co-created and a shared responsibility. Would it be possible to teach students about local, regional and national representation and affirming their identity as active agents who can make a difference?
3. Language learning is not a tool through which to engender shame and nurture the human propensity for categorization. How can we build on the richness of communities across the country by bringing languages into schools in a celebratory and empowering way?
4. Every child should have access to both the practice and appreciation of the arts (art, music, drama and theatre, dance). 'Art Collectives' could connect children with local issues and challenges by encouraging a creative response through the arts. How can we build and embed this new strand of learning into our schools?
5. Some of our schools need to be rebuilt to better hold and honour the health and well-being of our children and in a way that is both ecological and sustainable. Spaces for physical exercise (PE) within the school and in the community would better serve the talent and potential of future athletes and create the diverse talent pipeline into all sports that we seek. Would the major sports bodies and clubs be prepared to step up and contribute from their vast profits to fund and maintain these new spaces?
6. Secondary school science needs a new interdisciplinary body that brings together leading thinkers and educators to better connect the science taught in schools with local and global issues. Every secondary school should have a qualified and well-paid technician or team of technicians, and a fully resourced lab for practical science. Who will stand up for the school technicians and who will start this movement to bring earth and ecological sciences, and materials science into schools?
7. Geography has to be in 3D with the human and physical strands interwoven into a new subject that brings in geoscience and geopolitics, speaking to the climate crisis

and examining our relations to the different societal systems that we have created. Would it be possible to create a broader and even more sophisticated presentation of geography as a subject in schools?
8 School meals and free school meals are non-negotiable. FSM need to be expanded and children need to be properly fed. Additionally, what they eat should be the gateway to learning about 'farm to plate' and food journeys in which learning is encouraged and in which they can actively participate. How can we protect and promote the provision of good, healthy food for our children in schools?
9 History has to be inclusive and equally participatory. A new five-dimension teaching of history would develop contextual learning and bring history alive to learners, offering different entry points into themes and topics. What is stopping us from making the history curriculum more inclusive and richer?
10 A new integrative approach developed by researchers, educators and practitioners is needed for students with special educational needs and disabilities (SEND). The chronic lack of funding that forces every parent/carer to have to fight for the support, care and educational opportunities needed for their child must end. How can we build a new education system that tells students with SEND that they matter, and then shows it through practical support and positive educational experiences?

The education system cannot fix the challenges we face in society. The reality is that 'it may be that policymakers are looking in the wrong place and educational inequality might be better tackled not inside schools or families but by addressing poverty, and inequalities in health, housing and employment'.[4] Thus, it follows that some of the challenges faced in schools are the product of wider issues in society, which must be addressed.

This manifesto may seem frightening to some, and not bold enough for others. If the Covid-19 pandemic has shown us anything, it is that when our lives have already been turned upside down, this is not the time to go back to the way life used to be and accept it as the only way that life could be. This is as essential for challenging education inequality as it is for all other forms of social injustice. We can do better. We should envision a better education system. We must reimagine how we educate our children so that they can fully flourish and begin to step into the fullness of their being. Their futures rely on our courage.

Notes

1 Helen M. Gunter, 2012, *Leadership and the Reform of Education*, Bristol: Policy Press, p. 128.

2 Ian Abbott, David Middlewood, Sue Robinson, 2015, 'It's not just about value for money: A case study of values-led implementation of the Pupil Premium in outstanding schools', *Management in Education*, 29(4), pp. 178–84, p. 181.

3 Gemma Parker and David Leat, 2021, 'The Case of Curriculum Development in England: Oases in a Curriculum Desert' in Mark Priestley, Daniel Alvunger, Stavroula Philippou and Tiina Soini (eds), *Curriculum Making in Europe: Policy and Practice Within and Across Diverse Contexts*, Bingley: Emerald Publishing, pp. 151–74, p. 166.

4 Stephen J. Ball, 2017, *The Education Debate*, Bristol: Policy Press, p. 168.

Names and Subjects Index

Abbott, John 22–3
academy system
  classic disciplines and 143–4
Acts of the Apostles
  Spirit and languages 51
Alldred, Pam 153
Allen, Kim 25
Allport, Gordon 95
Andrew, Jesus calls to 20–2
arts
  creativity 87–9
  in curriculum 85–7
  embedding into schools 220
  importance of 79–81
  ousted from
    curriculum 79–80
  practicality and 98–100
  praise beyond words 76–8
  privileged few and 82–3
  reimagining 89–90
  at university 80
assembly
  character and 24–6
  reimagining 31–2
Association of School
  and College Leaders
  (ASCL) 116

Barker, John 153
Barr, Damian 188

Beadle, Philip 187–8
Birmingham, University
  of see Jubilee Centre for
  Character and Virtues
Black Cultural Archives 186
Black Education
  Movement 190
Black history 189–90
Black Lives Matter 42
Blair, Tony
  'Building Schools for the
    Future' 117–18
  PFI schemes and 116
Bradley, Kate 194
Braggs, Caroline, interview
  with 34–50
Bristow, Jane 168
Brooks, David
  The Road to Character 28–9
Bull, Anna 25

Cambridge University 54
Campaign for Science and
  Engineering (CaSE) 126,
  128
care, ethics of 155–6
Catholic education
  Benedictine 37
  Ignatian 37
  see also Braggs, Caroline

Centre for Information on
  Language Teaching and
  Research (CILT) 56–7, 58
character education
  assemblies and 24–6
  defining virtue 27–8
  historical perspective of
    26–31
  responsibility for 24–6
Chartered Institute of
  Linguists (CIOL) 71
Chartwells catering 169
Chefs in Schools 170
Child and Adolescent
  Mental Health Services
  (CAMHS) 48
Child Poverty Action Group
  171–2
Church of England
  Vision for Education 88
*Citizens Growing Up: At
  Home, At School and After*
  (Ministry of Education)
  27
citizenship 42, 220
class, social
  family experiences and 40
  'social mixing' in
    schools 8–9
Coard, Benjamin
  'How the West Indian Child
    is made Educationally Sub-
    Normal' 190
Collicutt, Red Canon
  Dr Joanna, interview
    with 93–108
Colvin, Marie 29
community
  geography and 161–2
  schools within 219

Conservative government
  policies
  curriculum and 11–12, 126,
    158–9
  PFI and 116
  politics in geography 157–8
  see also Gove, Michael
Convent of Jesus and Mary
  College 35, 53
Corinthians, Letter to
  value of the body 99
Council of Europe, language
  education and 55
Covid-19 pandemic
  creativity and 87
  demoralization from 45
  food insecurity and 172–4
  funding for schools 207–8
  highlights inequalities ix–x
  learning from 221–2
  medical careers interest and
    130
  PPE in schools 208
  practical science teaching
    and 133–4
  same storm, different boats
    188
  sports and 113–14
Cumberbatch, Syreeta 186
Cummins, Jim 64

dance, expression and 77
Davies, Jenny 206
Dearing (Sir Ron) Review 55
Dimbleby, Henry 169
drama, removed from
  curriculum 83–4
Duke University 80
Durham University, on
  creativity 87

NAMES AND SUBJECTS INDEX

education
  academic year structure 48–9
  author's experiences of 53–4
  current inequalities 5–10
  definitions of 96–9
  development of system 6–10
  'dustbin' schools 190–1
  exclusion 153–6
  flourishing within 3–5
  funding 39–41
  hope to do better ix–xi
  Jackson defines 144–5
  leadership 38–9
  learning beyond schools 219
  legislation 6–10
  lifelong 105–6
  opportunity 50
  pedagogy of care 155–6
  plurality of provision 9–10
  political decisions and 147
  reimagining 17–18, 218–22
  reward and motivation 95–6
  role and purpose of 22–3
  specialization/interdisciplinarian 97
  taking away choices 100–1
  'Education for All' (Swann Report) 189
education, health and care (EHC) plans 211–12, 214
Education, Ministry of
Citizens Growing Up 27
Education Reform Act (1988)
  curriculum objectives 158–9
  National Curriculum and 11–12
  science and 126
Elive, Francis 200
empty tomb 107–8

#EndChildFoodPoverty Task Force 172–3
English Baccalaureate (EBacc) 81, 187
English language
  as Additional Language (EAL) 61–5, 71
  reimagining learning of 70–1
  as a school subject 65–70
  'Standard' 69–70
Equiano, Olauda 185
Erasmus, Desiderius 3
ethnicity *see* race and ethnicity
examinations and testing
  England's programme of 89
  failing the 11-plus 101
  freeing children from 219
  grading system 204
  harms of 12–17
  maths 201–2, 204–5
  pandemic and 11, 45
  senior leadership team 205
  stress of 10
exclusion
  citizenship and 220
  race and ethnicity 153–4, 190–3

Faithful Companions of Jesus (FCJ) 34, 44
Finland, Helsinki library in 118–19
flourishing
  Braggs on 41–3
  defining 3
  exclusion and 155
  food and 174–6
  Jackson on 146–7

potential for children 3–5
SEND and 211–13
Food Foundation 173
A Framework for K-12 Science Education Practices, Crosscutting Concepts and Core Ideas (National Research Council) 132–3
free school meals 221
 pupil premium and 209–10
 sport and 112–13
 see also lunch; poverty
Freire, Paulo 155
French language 59
funding
 disparities in 205–9
 pupil premium 209–10, 214
 reimagining 214
 SEND 211–13, 218
Further Education Colleges 218

Gatsby Good Practical Science 134
gender
 geography and 159
 maths anxiety and 201–2
 science and 129
 sports participation and 113
 of teachers 94
geography
 ideology and curriculum 156–61
 new vision of 220–1
 power and exclusion 153–4
 reimagining teaching of 161–3
 school trips 150–2
German language 59

Gladwell, Malcolm
 Outliers 50
Goleman, Daniel 30
Gove, Michael
 changes curriculum 67–8, 86, 184
 exams and grading 204
 political agenda 147
 scraps Blair's plans 118–19
Grainger, Karen 70
Greek language 100
Guernica (Picasso) 78
Gulley, Frank 206
Gumley House school 34–50
Gypsy, Roma and Travellers bilingual children 63

Hackney School of Food 175
Hardy, G. H.
 A Mathematician's Apology 98
Harris, Professor Martin 55
headteachers, Braggs on 44–5
Hebrews, Letter to
 running the race 109
history
 of all 188–90
 Henry VIII 181–2
 the Holocaust 180–1
 independent schools 187–8
 moral portraits 182
 new vision for 221
 the prodigal son 178–80
 race and ethnicity 185–6, 189–90
 reimagining 194–5
 secondary school 186–90
 teachers 192–3
 what and why to teach 181–90

NAMES AND SUBJECTS INDEX

Holy Spirit, languages and 51–3
'How the West Indian Child is made Educationally Sub-Normal in the British School System' (Coard) 190
Huckle, John 160–2

imperialism, geography and 159–60
independent schools 187–8
inequalities
  current education and 5–10
  'dustbin' schools 190–1
  empowerment 65
  funding disparities 35, 205–9
  highlighted by pandemic ix
  Jackson on 147–8
  Nussbaum on 5
  pupil premium and 209–10
  school trips and 151–2
  SEND and 211–13
  'the good old days' and 188
  Zacchaeus and Jesus 198–9
Institute of Physics 133
International Charter on Geographical Education 160

Jackson, Professor Chris
  interview 138–48
James, son of Zebedee
  Jesus calls to 20–2
Jamie's School Dinners (television) 168
Jesus Christ
  calls to the fishermen 20–2
  the empty tomb 1–2

loaves and fishes 165–6
parable of the sower 149–50
the prodigal son 178–80
the race and 109–10
as role model 29
and Zacchaeus 198–9
John, Gospel of
  the empty tomb 1
John, son of Zebedee
  Jesus calls to 20–2
Joint Mathematical Council 202–3
Jubilee Centre for Character and Virtues 29–30
  'Character Education in UK Schools' 25–6
Junior English Revised (Richards) 53, 67

Kemp, Edward 84
King Jr, Martin Luther 23

Labour government policies 157–8
languages
  EAL: English as Additional 61–5
  effect of leaving EU and 60
  Holy Spirit and 51–3
  lesser-taught 59–60, 72
  MFL in secondary schools 54–60
  new vision of learning 220
  school trips and 150–1
  secondary school English 65–70
  three perspectives of 61
Lee, Harper
  To Kill a Mockingbird 68
Li Tim-Oi, Florence 189

lifelong learning 105–6
Local Government Association
  'Bright Futures' 211–12
Luke, Gospel of
  the prodigal son 178–9
  Zacchaeus and Jesus 198–9
lunch
  a child's responsibility and
    166–8
  food standards 168–70
  free school meals 170–4,
    221
  loaves and fishes 165–6
  new vision for 221
  reimagining school meals
    174–6
  school holidays 172–3

Macfarlane, Angus H. 156
MacTaggart, Heather 22–3
Madonna 29
Major, John, PFI schemes
  and 116
Mandela, Nelson, *Julius
  Caesar* quote and 84–5
Margrain, Valerie 156
Mark, Gospel of
  Jesus calls to followers 20
  parable of the sower
    149–50
Mary Magdalene, at the
  empty tomb 1–2
A Mathematician's Apology
  (Hardy) 98
mathematics
  anxiety and confidence
    199–202
  Jesus and Zacchaeus 198–9
  National Curriculum 202–5
  qualifications 202

  reimagining 214–15
Matthew, Gospel of
  loaves and fishes 165–6
Medical Schools Council 130
mental health 219
  counselling in schools 46–8
  distress in education 102–4
  maths anxiety 201–2
  school meals and 175
McQueen, Steve
  Small Axe 190
  Subnormal (documentary)
    191
Millar, Robin 134–5
Modern Foreign Languages
  (MFL) *see* languages;
  individual languages
'Morality in the 21st Century'
  (Sacks) 24
Murray, Pauli 189
music
  expression 77
  playing an instrument 78–9
  qualifications 81–2
  science and 99
  secondary schools 81–3
  'The State of Play' report 82
Music Industries Association
  82
Musicians' Union
  'The State of Play' report 82

National Association for
  Language Development In
  the Curriculum (NALDIC)
  71
  bilingual children and 63
National Association for
  the Teaching of English
  (NATE) 71

NAMES AND SUBJECTS INDEX

National Curriculum
  creativity and 87–9
  defining 'curriculum' 156–7
  English 66–71
  geography and 159–62
  history 183–90
  maths 202–5
  modern languages 55
  ousting the arts 79–80, 83–4
  PE 110–14
  reimagining 17
  science 126–8
  standard testing and 11–12
National Research Council
  *A Framework for K-12
  Science Education* 132–3
Nature journal, science
  teaching debate 130
Norway, education in 147
Nuffield Foundation,
  language learning 56
nursing, applications to 130
Nussbaum, Martha 5

Obama, Barack 29
Obama, Michelle 141
Of Mice and Men (Steinbeck)
  68
Ofsted
  inspection regime 13–14
  SEND children and 212
Oliver, Jamie
  Foundation 170
  Jamie's School Dinners 168
Organisation for Economic
  Co-operation and
  Development (OECD),
  PISA study 15–16
Osborne, Jonathan 134–5
Outliers (Gladwell) 50

Oxford University 94–5

Palmerston, Lord, on
  National Portrait Gallery
  182
Parks, Rosa 185
Paul of Damascus, focus on
  character 29
Personal Development, testing
  and 14
Personal, Social, Health
  and Economic (PSHE)
  programme
  mental health and 47
Peter (Simon)
  the empty tomb 1–2
  Jesus calls to 20–2
Physical Education (PE)
  see sports; National
  Curriculum
Picasso, Pablo
  Guernica 78
Pimlico Academy 144
politics
  character education and
    25–6
  see also Conservative
    government policies;
    Labour government
    policies; National
    Curriculum
poverty
  free school meals 170–4
  funding education and 40
  school trips and 151–2
  sports participation and 112
  structural change 199
  see also inequalities
Private Finance Initiative (PFI)
  schemes 115–18

229

Psalms
  heaven and earth 123
  praise the Lord 76
psychology
  Positive Psychology 29
  reward and motivation 95–6
pupil premium 209–10

qualifications
  art 86
  EBacc 81
  establishment 8
  history 186–8
  maths 202
  modern languages 54, 57–8
  Music BTEC 81–2
  reimagining 145–6
  science 126–7
Qualifications and Curriculum Development Agency (QCDA)
  modern language teaching 57–8

race and ethnicity
  BAME term 140
  bilingual students 61–5
  geography and 159–60
  history curriculum 185–6, 188–90
  history teachers 192–3
  labels 40
  potential and expectations 140–3
  Professor Smith's school years 138–40
  school exclusion and 153–4
  science and 129
  sports participation and 112

'Race, Ethnicity & Equality in UK History' (Royal Historical Society) 192–3, 194
Rashford, Marcus, child food poverty and 172–3
Rawding, Charles, politics and geography 157–8
resurrection, the empty tomb and 1–2
Richards, Hayden
  Junior English Revised 53–4, 67
  The Road to Character (Brooks) 28–9
Robinson, Marian 141
Royal Historical Society
  'Race, Ethnicity & Equality in UK History' 192–3, 194
Royal Society
  maths curriculum 202–3
  women and science 129
The Royal Society of Biology 133
The Royal Society of Chemistry 133
Ruiz, Richard, three perspectives of language 61

Sacks, Rabbi Jonathan
  on 'moral heroes' 29–30
  'Morality in the 21st Century' 24
School Food Matters 170
School Food Trust 170
school trips, helping parents 38
schools
  buildings and design 117–19, 152–3

NAMES AND SUBJECTS INDEX

as community 104–5
Covid and 208
exams competition 12
funding 205–9
independent 187–8
inspection regime 13–14
new vision of 220
PFI schemes and 115–18
prison-like 116–17, 119
space for sport 114–19
swimming pools 115
science
 content of learning 132–5
 heaven and earth 123–4
 Jackson on 143–4
 old and new challenges for 134–5
 reimagining 135–6, 220
 in schools 125–30
 STEM pathway 76, 127–8
 teaching debate 130–2
 technicians 129–30
Seacole, Mary 185
Seligman, Martin E. P. 30
sexuality, mental health and 47–8
Shakespeare, William
 Julius Caesar and Mandela 84–5
Shamji, Irfan 84
Shannon, Lyttanya
 Subnormal (documentary) 191
Sign Supported English (SSE) 67–70
Small Axe (film anthology) 190
Sodexo Education 168
Solnit, Rebecca x–xi
Spanish Civil War 78

Spanish language 59
Special Educational Needs and Disabilities (SEND)
 funding for 211–13
 new vision for 221
 sports and 112
Sport England Active Partnerships 114
sports
 netball 110–11
 PE And Sports Survey 112–13
 PFI schemes and 115–18
 the race 109–10
 reimagining 119–21
 school buildings and 220
 secondary school PE 110–14
 spaces for 114–19
 swimming 115
 tennis 120
'The State of Play' (Musicians' Union report) 82
Steinbeck, John
 Of Mice and Men 68
Subnormal (documentary) 191
Sussex University School of Education and Social Work 81
Sutton Trust, science teachers and 128
Swann Report
 'Education for All' 189
Swords, Rachel 70

teachers
 confidence 39
 exam system and 13–17
 gender of 94
 history 192–3

231

reimagined education 17–18
science 128–30
Tempest, Kate 29
Temple Sutton Primary
 School, Southend 206
Templeton (John) Foundation
 26
Thatcher, Margaret 29, 184
theology, practical 96, 98,
 100
Thevenet, Claudine 35
*The Times Educational
 Supplement*
 funding disparities 205–6
 'The Problem with character
 education' 24–5
To Kill a Mockingbird
 (Lee) 68
Tomlinson, Carol Ann 10

UK Music 82
United Nations Convention
 on the Rights of the Child
 155
United States
 civil rights movement 191
 history as subject 187
 science teaching 133
universities
 fellowship 107

learning as commodity
 106–7

Vincent, John 169

Watson, Emma 29
Wellcome Trust 127
Westborough School,
 Southend 206
Westwell, John 205
Wheeler, Rebecca S. 70
Wilkin, Rose-Hudson 189
Williamson, Gavin 80
Winkett, Lucy 189
World Health Organization
 175

young people
 into adulthood 43
 bilingual 61–5
 new vision of education
  218–22
 purpose of education 22–3
 role models for 29
 shame and 146–7
Youth Sport Trust 113

Zacchaeus 198–9

www.ingramcontent.com/pod-product-compliance
Lightning Source LLC
Chambersburg PA
CBHW022050290426
44109CB00014B/1046